The Pro

The Pro

Lessons from My Father

About Golf and Life

CLAUDE "BUTCH" HARMON, JR.

with STEVE EUBANKS

THREE RIVERS PRESS • NEW YORK

I would like to dedicate this book to my loving family: my brothers, Craig, Dick, and Bill, who in the writing of this book revived so many special memories for me; my children, C.H., Michaele, and Cole, who keep me young through the wonder of their lives; and finally, my dearest wife, Christy, who is the very air that I breathe. My love and thanks to each of you.

Copyright © 2006 by Claude "Butch" Harmon, Jr.

All rights reserved.

Published in the United States by Three Rivers Press, an imprint of the
Crown Publishing Group, a division of Random House, Inc., New York.
www.crownpublishing.com

Three Rivers Press and the Tugboat design are registered trademarks
of Random House, Inc.

Originally published in hardcover in the United States of America by
Crown Publishers, a division of Random House, Inc., in 2006.

Library of Congress Cataloging-in-Publication Data
Harmon, Claude "Butch," 1943–
The pro: lessons from my father about golf and life / Claude "Butch"
Harmon, Jr. with Steve Eubanks.—1st ed.   1. Harmon, Claude "Butch,"
1943–   2. Harmon, Claude, 1916–1989   3. Golfers—United States—
Biography.   4. Fathers and sons—United States.
I. Eubanks, Steve, 1962–   II. Title.
GV964.H3A3   2006
796.352092–dc22   2006003963

ISBN 978-0-307-33804-4

Printed in the United States of America

Design by Leonard Henderson

10   9   8   7   6   5   4   3   2   1

First Paperback Edition

Contents

The Pro

Introduction

Passing the Pearls

I don't remember the first time I heard it: that booming voice erupting from the barrel-chested, bigger-than-life man who dominated my life.

"These are pearls I'm giving you," my father would say as he stared through the backs of my eyes and pointed his meaty finger in my direction, never threatening but like a maestro conducting the final movement of a symphony. "Pearls! Not everybody gets these! Pay attention!"

We were standing on the driving range at Winged Foot, the thirty-six–hole golf club in Mamaroneck, New York, twenty-five minutes from the city and one of the greatest championship golf clubs in the world, host of the 1929, 1959, 1974, and 2006 U.S. Opens, the 1957 U.S. Women's Open, the 1997 PGA Championship, and the 2004 U.S. Amateur Championship. My father, the man "passing the pearls" to his sons that afternoon, was the pro. Today's pearl: practice.

"You don't practice a golf swing, you practice golf shots," he said, the finger waving as the symphony reached a crescendo. "You can stand out here all day working on this position or that, but if you aren't working on golf shots, you're wasting your time. I don't work on anything I'm not going to need on the back nine on a Sunday."

At that stage in my life I didn't say "Blah, blah, blah" out loud, because I knew it would have earned me swift and well-deserved corrective measures, but I wasn't listening, either. Like most sons, particularly those like me, who were bestowed with their fathers' names, there were many years when I found my dad to be an irrepressible bore, a know-it-all who had me rolling my eyes and yawning during his predictable, well-trodden speeches. What I didn't realize that afternoon was just how prophetic and wise my father's words were and how often I would use them later on in life.

"Purpose! Purpose!" he said, punching each word with the finger. "If you aren't out here practicing with a purpose, you might as well be playing tiddly-winks. Everything you do out here has to be for a reason. If you're going through the motions, go do something else, because you're wasting your time and taking up a spot on the range that somebody else—somebody serious—could be using."

At this point I gazed down the first fairway of the West Course at a group of members who had just teed off, my mind a million miles away from the message—"the pearl"—being laid out for me.

"Every shot must be played for a reason," my father continued, even though I knew he could see that he'd lost me. "Just beating balls with a pretty swing might impress the twenty-handicap members, but it's not doing you one bit of good when it comes to playing golf. If you're out here hitting high, straight six-irons, posing pretty for the ladies, what are you going to do when you get to the third tee and have to cut a low three-iron into a hurting wind?"

Okay, this wasn't the kind of lesson Dad would have given those same twenty-handicap members who kept his appointment book full. I knew that I was getting something from him that he didn't give to most, something that could be called a "pearl" if you were so inclined, which my father was. I still couldn't have cared less. The members on the first fairway were about to hit their second shots, and a male cardinal lit in a tree beside the putting green. My dad might as well have been prattling on about the weather.

Out of frustration, Dad dug his big hand deep into the pocket of his slacks and pulled out a bulging money clip. He always carried stupid amounts of cash, having upwards of a thousand dollars on him at any given time. This was the case even back in the sixties, when a thousand dollars would buy a freshly painted and well-running used Mustang and put a substantial down payment on a house. Maybe it came from his experiences in the Great Depression, although we never talked about it, but he believed that a man should always have cash. When my three brothers and I were young, he would insist that we never leave the house with less than five dollars in our pockets. We weren't supposed to spend the money—in fact, there was a full accounting of what we spent every night—but we had to carry it. "A man's got to have cash," he would say. "You never know when you'll need it."

This day, with a cool north wind predicting the end of another New York golf season, my father tossed the money clip to the ground with a quick flick of the wrist. Then he pulled a five-iron out of his golf bag, took a couple of practice swings, and began the same pre-shot ritual I had watched my entire life. I'd seen it millions of times on the range, thousands of times during rounds where I either followed him or carried his golf bag, and during dozens of professional tournaments where I had walked side-by-side with my father as he competed against the likes of Ben Hogan, Byron Nelson, and Sam Snead.

The routine never varied. From a spot behind the ball, he took the club in his left hand and then in his right. His hands were unique—thick and leathery with so many calluses they felt like the scratchy weathered masts of a giant sailing ship. Like most golf pros of his generation, Dad had built his own game from scratch, finding the fundamentals in countless trials and failures that showed in each crease on his palms. I had felt those hands many times as they held me when I was young, and when they hugged me days and nights well into adulthood. My father never shied away from physical affection with his sons, and we never thought twice about hugging and kissing him every day of his life. When placed on a golf club, however, the rough-hewn hands took on a softer, more artistic flair. Dad gripped a club the way Miles Davis held a muted horn—like an appendage, no different from a third arm. It was a part of him.

His eyes were his second-most indelible feature. Caribbean hazel and intense, all the Harmon boys could read his feelings by looking there. When he gripped the club, those eyes focused on the position of his hands as if he were a surgeon performing a risky procedure. Because of joint problems he'd had since childhood, my dad wrapped his left thumb around the grip rather than running it straight down the shaft, as is customary. As a result his left-hand grip looked more like Ted Williams holding a baseball bat than Ben Hogan gripping a golf club. I never saw him teach that grip to anyone else, but it worked for him for half a century. I'm still convinced he could have hit a five-iron blindfolded in his sleep at midnight and nothing would have been different, it came so naturally to him. But that didn't stop him from concentrating on his hands as they wrapped around the grip of the club. Then he put the clubhead behind the ball before placing his right foot and then his left in position. Two waggles of the club, and then his eyes moved slowly between the ball and the line of his intended shot.

Usually he was ready to swing. But this time he hesitated. Without taking his eyes off the target, he said, "Do you see those flags?"

I looked down the range, and along with my brothers, acknowledged the row of flags.

"If I hit one shot left of those flags, you boys can split everything in that money clip."

With that, he swung the club, and the ball flew from the ground with a crisp click. It sailed up into the deep blue sky on a perfect line, and a perfect trajectory, over the first flag, then the second, until it reached its apex. Then it drifted ever so slightly, falling five yards right of the third flag in the line. A few seconds later, another shot flew on exactly the same path; then a third, then a fourth, a fifth, and a sixth.

At the time, I didn't fully see the "pearl" my father had passed along to me that afternoon, but the one thing I knew for certain was that we Harmon brothers were more likely to be abducted by aliens than get a dime of the money in that clip. I questioned my father about a lot of things when I was young, but the one aspect of his life I knew better than to underestimate was his ability to hit one perfect golf shot after another. None of those balls was going left of the flags, and every one of us knew it.

Claude Harmon, my father, had the kind of natural golf talent that made him a prodigy. At age thirteen, he shot sixty-three at Dubs Dread in Orlando in an exhibition with two of the game's greats, Walter Hagen and Gene Sarazen. He qualified for the U.S. Amateur at fourteen, and in the 1940s, after turning pro, he won the Miami Fourball, the Havana Open twice, the Westchester Open three times, the National Championship of Club Professionals, and the Met PGA. He finished in the top five in nine major championships, made it to the semifinals of the PGA Championship three times (the event was match-play at the time), and finished third in the 1959 U.S. Open, the highest finish in the national open by a club pro in the modern era. And also, in 1948, when I was four years old, my father produced his best-ever performance, shooting a tournament-record nine-under-par at Augusta National to win the Masters tournament by five shots.

Dad was the last club pro ever to win a major, the final member of an extinct breed: the workingman champion, the playing club pro. He came into the business at a time when there were barely three thousand golf courses in America, mostly consisting of one-tractor operations in one-stoplight towns where no pro was needed. Today there are more than sixteen thousand golf facilities and more than sixty thousand men and women who call themselves golf professionals. Unfortunately, my father closed the door on the golden age of golf pros, an age that dated back to Old Tom Morris, who ran a shop in St. Andrews in Scotland and

taught the game to the nobility of the day when he wasn't winning championships. What Tom Morris started, Dad finished. He
was the last club pro to compete regularly in all three major championships contested on U.S. soil, and he was the last to become
world-renowned for both his teaching and his playing ability. I
would argue that Dad was the greatest teacher the game has ever
seen. For sure he was the greatest father a man could ever have.

Dad possessed a unique skill set, one that is hard to find in
the modern-day golf pro. Today, most major-championship–
caliber players lack the "giving" skills necessary to be good teachers. Not that they are selfish people—the vast majority are not—but
to be a great player, you have to be a little insular and egotistical.
Let's face it, when you make your living rolling in ten-foot birdie
putts, you have to live in a world where most everything is about
"you, you, you." Being a great teacher not only requires empathy,
it also takes someone who wants nothing more out of life than
the satisfaction that comes from helping others. My father possessed both. He could take an average golfer to the lesson tee, and
within five or ten minutes the student would be making better
swings and hitting more solid golf shots. Later that afternoon, he
might take Sam Snead, Tommy Armour, or Johnny Revolta out
onto the West Course at Winged Foot and close them out on a
fifty-dollar match before the sixteenth tee.

Dad could make any student play better if he was willing to
listen. Fortunately, his playing record and reputation as a teacher
left him no shortage of those. Dad taught golf to kings and presidents, and captains of industry, as well as to past and future tour
players and major championship winners. In the process, he revo-
lutionized teaching, using such technology as eight-millimeter film
projection, which not only allowed students to see their swings in

slow motion and stills but also to compare their swings with all the great golfers of the day—a radical way of teaching golf in the pre–*I Love Lucy* era. He is the only teaching pro ever to be on the cover of *Sports Illustrated,* not because of his playing prowess but because of his unique ability to communicate the fundamentals of the golf swing. He was one of the first to use a weighted golf club as a training aid. He had a driver with so much lead in the head that the thing must have weighed nine pounds. "I swung that club a hundred times a day to get my hands strong," I heard him tell many students. "If you're serious about getting better, you can swing it as often as possible." Years before you could order swing-connection devices through toll-free numbers off late-night infomercials, Dad was taking the belt off his trousers and wrapping it around the upper arms and torsos of students who needed to tighten their swings. He did this for good players, bad players, rich and poor. He did it in New York, Florida, Texas, California, and anywhere else anyone needed a helping hand with his golf swing. He did it to make people better. He did it because he cared.

He taught Presidents Eisenhower, Kennedy, Nixon, and Ford; he was the personal instructor to King Hassan II of Morocco and the recipient of the Moroccan Medal of Honor, the nation's highest award. He taught Henry Ford, the Duke of Windsor, Bob Hope, Randolph Scott, Howard Hughes (yes, *that* Howard Hughes), Bing Crosby, Lana Turner, Johnny Carson, and just about every other celebrity who trekked to South Florida or Palm Springs for the winter. He also offered advice freely and openly to his fellow competitors. During a U.S. Open practice round, Dad and Mr. Hogan were playing with U.S. Open champion Dr. Cary Middlecoff. When Cary failed to get out of his third bunker in a row, Dad turned to Mr. Hogan and said, "Ben, I've got to help

Doc with his bunker play. He's the worst I've ever seen." To which, Mr. Hogan said, "Leave him alone, Claude. If we're lucky, he'll never learn." Dad gave Middlecoff the lesson anyway.

He coached and trained forty-four assistant professionals, including Jackie Burke, who won sixteen tour events, two majors, and captained a Ryder Cup team; Mike Souchak, who won sixteen times and held the professional seventy-two-hole scoring record on tour for forty years before one of my students, Mark Calcavecchia, broke it in 2001; Dick Mayer, who was Winged Foot's first junior member and learned the game exclusively from my father before going on to win the 1957 U.S. Open and World Golf Championship; Dave Marr, winner of the 1965 PGA Championship and another Ryder Cup captain; and Rod Funseth, four-time regular tour and two-time senior tour winner. He also trained pros like Al Mengert, who won the 1960 Metropolitan Open before becoming the head professional at Oakland Hills Country Club, where he remained for fourteen years, and Jack Lumpkin, who played the tour in the seventies before becoming the director of golf instruction at Sea Island, where he is consistently ranked among the top fifty golf instructors in the world.

Along the way, Claude Harmon taught his four irascible sons to play the game, too. He also taught us how to live. And while the lines between golf lessons and life lessons blurred sometimes, there was never a question that my father was right about the "pearls" he was passing along to us. They were, indeed, special. And not everybody could get them.

It's not unusual for a son to follow in his father's professional footsteps. The world is full of second-generation lawyers, doctors, bankers, developers, and even golf pros. It is somewhat unusual when four sons choose the same career path as their father, as my brothers and I have done. We all teach golf for a living, and we have all done well within our profession. Those who rank such things have consistently placed me, Craig, Dick, and Billy among the top-fifty golf instructors in the world. My brother Craig has been the PGA Club Professional of the Year and remains the head pro at Oak Hill in Rochester, New York. My brother Dick, who passed away suddenly and unexpectedly in February 2006, owned his own golf school in Houston, Texas, and taught many great tour players. He was widely recognized as one of the greatest young-golfer coaches in the world. Billy was the head professional at Newport Country Club before moving back to Palm Springs. He is currently the Director of Instruction at Toscana Country Club and still caddies for his close friend, Jay Haas, on the PGA Tour. And I have a golf school in Las Vegas and have been ranked the number-one golf instructor in the world for several years running.

I bring this up not to boast but to make a point: no matter how much we have accomplished in our careers, or how much we will accomplish in the future, none of the Harmon boys is, or ever will be, half the teacher our father was. We all agree on this fact, and we are all reminded of it with every lesson we give. My brother Billy says, "Every lesson I give, I think, 'Now, what would Dad say?'" and my brother Dick says, "I've never given a lesson where he wasn't the benchmark." As for me, whether I'm coaching a major championship winner at a PGA Tour event or helping an eighteen-handicap woman who's having trouble getting a ball airborne with her driver, I never give a lesson without thinking of my father. Most times, I find myself repeating the same words to my students that I once heard from him.

•   •   •

Dad fought a hook when he was young—a low, screaming right-to-left golf shot that had trouble written on it from the moment it left the club. Sometimes his timing was perfect and he played the shot beautifully, starting it well right of his intended target and curving it into play. Sometimes his timing was a little off, and he would hit shots so far left he was lucky to find the ball. It wasn't until he came to Winged Foot as an assistant that he learned the pitfalls of hitting it left. Craig Wood, winner of the 1941 Masters, U.S. Open, and Canadian Open, was the head professional at the time. He told my father, "Claude, you can play pretty well in this state with that shot. You'll win a few local events. And you can play with these members. They'll be impressed with you. But you'll never beat the best players in the world with a hook." So, Dad spent the rest of his playing days working on eliminating the right-to-left shot from his repertoire.

"Ben Hogan told me that it wasn't the hook that kills you, it's the fear of hitting it," Dad said, unfazed by dropping the name of the greatest ball-striker the game has ever known. Why would he? They were friends. Mr. Hogan played more major-championship practice rounds with my father than with any other player in the game. They would practice together in Florida in the winters, play all their practice rounds together, and play friendly matches whenever they could. In their standard game, hitting the fairway was worth a point, hitting the green was worth another point, closest to the pin was worth a point, three-putting took away a point, and the lowest score on each hole was worth a point. Each point was worth ten dollars. "Talk about learning course management: try playing fairways and greens with Ben Hogan for ten dollars a shot," Dad would say. My father was the only pro Mr. Hogan would listen to when it came to the swing, and of course, Dad would listen to anything Mr. Hogan had to say. I only wish I had been as willing to listen to my father that afternoon as Mr. Hogan had been throughout his career.

"We can stand here all day; not one of them's going left," he said as another five-iron shot soared over the flags and fell softly to the right of the line. Even though I knew he was right, I couldn't take my eyes off him as he hit shot after shot just right of the flags. The man's talents with a golf club were unparalleled. He could have stood there all day and never hit a ball left of his intended target, or even off-line. He also could have walked into any one of the cavernous bunkers at Winged Foot and holed one out of every three sand shots he hit. I'd seen him do it too many times. For years, he would end his short-game clinics in the bunker by saying, "Okay, now I'm going to end by holing one for you." And he would! During the member-guest tournaments, as members, guests, and spouses enjoyed cocktails on the terrace outside Winged Foot's famous grill, Dad would walk into one of the crater bunkers guarding the eighteenth green of the East Course, throw down a handful of balls, and say, "If anybody's interested, I'm paying two-to-one that I can hole one of these." He never lost, and the members never stopped betting him. Everyone had a great time.

Jackie Burke, who worked for Dad as an assistant at Winged Foot before going on to win the Masters and PGA Championship in 1956, tells a great story about Dad's sand play. "Nobody swung the club any better than Claude Harmon," Jackie said. "I can't tell you the number of times I was playing him when I'd hit an approach into the middle of a green and have a twenty-footer for birdie, and he'd miss the green in the bunker. He'd always say, 'All right, Jackie, you can give me the tie right now, or we'll play this hole out for an extra dollar.' I'd take the bet, and he'd hole that bunker shot almost every time."

Thirty-plus years after watching my dad hit one five-iron after another right of those flags on the range at Winged Foot, I was in Las Vegas when my thoughts flooded back to that breezy autumn afternoon. It was October 1996, a virtual eternity from the day my dad bet us all the money in his pocket that he wouldn't hit a single shot left of those flags. I found myself passing along Claude's "pearls" to my star student of the day, a young new pro named Tiger Woods. The weather at Winged Foot that afternoon probably wasn't much different than it had been that afternoon three decades before. But in Las Vegas, it was hot and dry, a pressure-cooker of a Sunday and a fantastic time to be part of what the media was calling "Team Tiger."

At the time, I had been teaching Tiger for four years, although I hadn't actually spent as much face-to-face time with him during that period as most people thought. Because he had just turned pro and I was working at a club, we did most of our work over the telephone and through video when he was an amateur. Tiger would overnight tapes to me, and we would talk about them over the phone. I would see him at the majors, and the few amateur events I frequented (mainly the U.S. Amateur). Other than that, we had been long-distance companions. After becoming the first player in history to win three consecutive U.S. Amateur titles, Tiger announced in Milwaukee that he was turning pro, amid a media frenzy that hadn't been seen in sports since Ali–Frazier four decades before. Every event Tiger played in those last weeks of 1996 was like a presidential campaign stop, complete with harried reporters and daily updates on such inane minutiae as what the kid ate for dinner and which video games he enjoyed most.

By the time we got to Vegas the circus had grown to laughable proportions. Tiger was twenty years old—he couldn't legally play a hand of blackjack at his hotel (a fact he learned the hard way when he was carded on the gaming floor at the MGM Grand). Yet he garnered more media attention than any golfer in history, and all before he won a professional event!

He'd been a professional only six weeks. The Las Vegas Invitational was the fifth of seven sponsor's exemptions Tiger had accepted. Since the PGA Tour didn't hand out membership cards based on potential, Tiger had accepted these sponsor's exemptions in the hope of earning enough money to finish the year in the top 125 on the money list. That would automatically qualify him as a member for 1997 and exempt him from Tour Qualifying School.

I had a feeling that earning his card wouldn't be a problem. Tiger had risen to the top in everything he'd ever tried. He'd been the best junior golfer in the world, the best amateur golfer in the world, and I felt certain that he would become the best professional golfer in the world. What I didn't expect, and what I think caught a lot of people off guard, was just how fast Tiger proved himself among the best players in the game. That Sunday afternoon in the desert, Tiger shot sixty-four in the final round. When he tapped in on the final hole, he held a one-shot lead.

I waited behind the eighteenth green with some advice. "Don't celebrate yet," I told him. "And don't talk to the media. You're probably going to be in a playoff with Davis Love III."

An enormous crowd of reporters waited behind the eighteenth green with cameras, microphones, and pens in hand. I steered Tiger away from them, and we headed to the driving range. If Davis got in with one more birdie, there would be a playoff. The tournament wasn't over. Tiger needed to stay in the same mindset he'd been in on the course.

At the driving range, he hit a few warm-up shots just to keep his shoulders loose, then without being prompted, he went to his bag and pulled out a three-wood. The first playoff hole was a par four. He'd hit driver there every day. On the range he teed up the three-wood and hit a few balls with a hard fade—a driving, controlled shot that would split the middle of any fairway. That's when I realized what he was doing. Davis was a long hitter, one of the longest in the game, but at the time nobody realized how far Tiger Woods hit the golf ball. Nobody, in fact, came close to hitting it as far as Tiger. That was why Tiger was hitting his three-wood. If it came to a playoff, he wanted his opening tee shot to be in the fairway, but behind Davis's ball. That would allow him to play first. If he stuck the ball close to the hole, he could get the viewing gallery into it and shift the momentum his way.

It was a masterful strategy, one that showed a level of maturity I could never have imagined from a twenty-year-old. If any other rookie had found himself waiting for a sudden-death playoff in his sixth tour start, I daresay he might have had trouble figuring out which end of the club to hold. Tiger not only knew what he needed to do but he also had a particular shot in mind for the playoff, a shot that would set up a second shot. He was thinking three shots ahead, even before he knew the playoff would take place!

As he hit another three-wood, and then another, I thought back to that afternoon at Winged Foot with my father, and the "pearl" he had shared with his sons. "Purpose! Purpose!" Tiger had it. Every shot he hit in practice was struck with the intent of accomplishing something. He never practiced golf swings; he worked on golf shots. In this case, the tee shot he needed to hit on the first playoff hole of the first professional tournament he had a chance to win.

The strategy almost backfired. Davis shot sixty-seven, and did, indeed, tie Tiger for the lead at the end of regulation. But when they marched out to the eighteenth for the playoff, Tiger was so pumped up he almost flew his three-wood shot past Davis's driver. Still, Tiger played first and hit his approach onto the green. When Davis pulled his approach into the rough and failed to get up-and-down for par, the tournament was over.

I was amazed. I thought it would take at least three or four months for Tiger to make the transition and become a winner on the PGA Tour. (Turns out he won twice in his first eight weeks and qualified for the season-ending Tour Championship.) After his playoff victory in Las Vegas I doubled over laughing when the showgirls, wearing fandango headwear and little else, presented him with the trophy and the $295,000 check. He looked like a kid caught peeping through Hugh Hefner's keyhole.

Half an hour later, Tiger sat in the pressroom answering questions while I went into the locker room at the TPC at Summerlin to gather up the few things he'd left behind. The staff congratulated me, which brought on another laugh. There was no need to congratulate me. I hadn't struck a shot all week. But I thanked them, anyway.

That's when it dawned on me that Tiger hadn't tipped the locker room staff. He was twenty, and even though he'd signed contracts worth north of $40 million, he still lived and acted like a college student. Tipping, an appropriate and expected practice on tour, hadn't occurred to him. So I gave the head locker room attendant $300, not enough by any stretch, but all the cash I had on me at the time.

A few minutes later I climbed into the back of the limo for the short trip back to the MGM Grand. "Tiger," I said, "you owe me three hundred bucks."

"What for?" he asked.

"I tipped the locker room staff."

"You gave them three hundred dollars!"

"Yeah. I would have given them more, but that's all I had. I emptied my pockets."

"For what?"

"Tiger, those guys took care of your stuff all week. They busted their butts in there."

"Yeah?" he said, not quite believing me.

That's when I realized just how much Tiger had to learn, not about golf but about how the world worked.

"Tiger," I said, keeping my voice as calm as I could. "You just won close to three hundred thousand dollars. You should have tipped them a grand. And you should do the same thing every week, win or lose. Every Tuesday when you show up, you should hand out hundreds to everybody in the locker room and thank them in advance for taking care of you. The more successful you are, the more you're going to have to rely on others for the basics—looking after your stuff, getting you around, keeping you from being mobbed. If you take care of those people, they'll take care of you. Never forget the folks on the sidelines. They're the ones who keep your world turning."

Then I thought about my father's money clip and words he pounded home to me on more than a few occasions. "And always keep cash in your pockets," I said. "You need to carry a good amount of money around, because you never know who you'll need to tip or what you'll need to buy."

Tiger nodded his head, but it was me who was smiling. I had first gotten that same speech in a lot less friendly tone of voice when I was thirteen years old. I had trotted out to the course one morning full of misplaced arrogance and stupidity, but ready to play anyway. One of the caddies retrieved my bag from storage, and I noticed that he had cleaned my clubs. Without a word, I took the bag and headed toward the first tee. Before I could put a peg in the ground, Dad marched out of the shop and got within inches of my face.

"Why didn't you tip that caddy?" he barked, the big finger under my chin punching each word.

"I didn't bring any money," I said. This seemed logical enough to me. I was thirteen.

"If you can't afford to tip the people who clean your clubs, you don't need to have them cleaned," he said. "And what about a thank-you? Could you not afford that, either?"

I just hung my head.

"Listen," Dad said, as if I had another option. "No matter where you go in life, you're never to forget the little guys, because when you're one of them, you don't want people forgetting about you."

"Yes, sir."

"And if you're down to your last dollar, give it to the guy who helps you out. You can make more money. You can never make up for slighting a man."

In Las Vegas, I didn't go that far with Tiger. I didn't have to. He is as sharp as they come. He got it.

I passed a lot of my father's pearls of wisdom to Tiger in the ten years he and I worked together. But that was nothing new. I've shared my father's insights with every student I've ever taught, and will continue to do so in every lesson I give. A lot of Dad's tips that I've passed along have helped golfers improve their games; some have helped players hone their focus and let their natural talents shine through; some have had nothing to do with golf. A lot of Dad's advice was intended to help people through rough spots in their lives. I've passed those pearls along as well. No matter what I've said on the lesson tee, or to the golfing public at large, one thing is certain: every ounce of wisdom and every tip I've ever uttered have come from the same source—one of the finest golfers of his generation, and one of the greatest teachers of the game who ever lived: The Pro, my father, Claude Harmon.

"If It Were Easy,
Everybody Would Do It"

"Golf is hard!"

Dad used to lurch forward with his arms out as he made this proclamation. While a little less than six feet tall, Dad was always big, a thick man with broad shoulders and a wide neck. When he lunged to make a point, he looked like a blitzing linebacker. His hands would go wide as if he were about to make a tackle. Then he would say,

"Golf's hard. Good golf is damn hard, and championship golf is so hard only a select few ever comprehend it. It's a cruel game. Think about it. A hundred and forty-four people play in the tournament, and a hundred and forty-three of them are going to lose. That's tough. The game chews you up, spits you out, and steps on you. It's those who get up and dust themselves off that make it. But that's how it should be. If it were easy, everybody would do it."

Dad pounded this point home to me and my brothers on

more occasions than any of us can remember. He didn't always use the same words. One of his favorite expressions, for example, was, "Show me somebody who is practicing for today, and I'll show you somebody who has no chance of getting better tomorrow." This was another way of saying the same thing. Golf is hard. It takes a lot of work. If you want to play good golf, you had better be willing to put in long, hard hours, for an extended period of time. And in many cases, you have to get worse before you can get better.

My brothers and I knew he was right. To say "golf is hard" is like saying "the sky is blue" or "the world is round." It's axiomatic, which made Dad's passion for repeating it seem odd at times. I wanted to say things like, "Yeah, sure, Dad, okay, it's hard, so what does my spine angle look like at impact?" But he would never let us forget the point. Dad made sure we understood that golf was not a game you ever perfected. The moment you thought you had golf whipped, the game slapped you down and embarrassed you. Conversely, whenever you were ready to quit forever, a good thought and a good round came along and sparked the smoldering ember of hope.

He also drummed the message that golf was not a game of steady progressions. You don't get 10 percent better in the first six months and 10 percent better every month after that. Nor was it a game where results tied directly to one component, like talent or repetitions. One golfer might hit five hundred balls a day for a decade and never break par, while another might put his clubs away for months and shoot in the sixties in his first outing. Champion golfers were those who had talent on top of spending endless hours on the practice tees.

I knew all of this—all the Harmon boys did—but knowing that

the game is unyielding, unfair, unpredictable, unsympathetic, and unaware of who you are and what you shot yesterday, and accepting such truths are two different things. Plenty of times, I wanted the quick fix, the magic potion that would make my game better by noon. My father had little patience for those, like me, who looked for easy answers. "The tip-of-the-day pro is the one I want to be playing against," he would say.

He also had little use for anyone who thought the golf swing had to feel "good" or "natural." My youngest brother Billy, who as a teenager was one of the best junior players in the country, used to argue with Dad about how a change "felt." When Dad tried to change Billy's grip to keep him from hitting an occasional hook, Billy said, "Dad, it doesn't feel right."

My father snatched up the ball and club and held both within inches of Billy's face. "You see that ball?" he barked.

"Yes, sir," Billy said.

"And you see that club?"

"Yes, sir."

"Well, that ball and that club are inanimate objects. *In-an-i-mate!* The ball is only going to do what the club makes it do, and the club is only going to go where you swing it. Neither of them gives a damn how you feel."

I never heard him use that kind of language with any students whose last names weren't Harmon, but he was always most direct when appraising our games. If we opted for the easy road instead of making the fundamental changes necessary to get better, he would let us know about it in his own special way. Once he was watching Billy on a day when our youngest brother thought his swing couldn't get much better. Each shot was solid, and the balls were flying long and straight on a perfect trajectory. He waited for

Dad to say something like, "Wow, you're really hitting it great," or "That swing looks perfect." When no praise came, Billy finally asked, "What are you thinking about, Dad?"

Dad said, "I'm thinking about P. T. Barnum, and the Ringling brothers."

This put Billy in a bind. He wanted to know what Dad thought, but he knew the Ringling and Barnum reference was a precursor to a dig. So, my brother took a deep breath and said, "Okay, Dad, what about them?"

"Well, you know, Barnum and those guys travel over to Africa to get these elephants for their shows. They get them young, spend time with them, and train them."

"Yeah?" Billy said.

"Well, those they can't train, they ship back to Africa."

Still waiting for a point, Billy said, "So?"

Dad shook his head and said, "I've got no place to send you."

This didn't sit well with my brother, who felt like he was hitting the ball as well as he had all season. "Why can't you say something positive?" he asked.

"I can when you do something positive. As long as you jerk the club to the inside on your takeaway [a swing flaw Billy fought throughout his playing days], it doesn't matter how good you hit it today, you're never going to be a golfer."

Billy wasn't thrilled, but Dad couldn't have cared less. The swing wouldn't last, so as far as Dad was concerned, it didn't matter how well Billy hit it. If he was unwilling to sacrifice the good feeling of a solid shot today for the hard work and bad shots that were bound to accompany a much-needed swing change, then he was like an uncoachable elephant. The fact that the swing worked once in a while was of no consequence. If you couldn't repeat it under pressure, as Dad assured Billy he could not, then it didn't matter.

When my brother Craig was getting ready to qualify for the U.S. Open, Dad took him out to the West Course at Winged Foot to see his game. Craig felt pretty good about himself. He'd been practicing all summer, and he had talked about how this was his year. He even felt confident enough to challenge our father to a little game. Craig played as good as he could and shot a seventy-one. Dad, well into his fifties at that point and suffering from the early stages of arthritis, shot a seven-birdie round of sixty-five.

Craig couldn't believe it. "Dad, I just played as good as I can play and shot seventy-one," he said. "I didn't think there was a sixty-five out there. How'd you do that?"

Dad put his arm around Craig and said, "It's really simple, son. Some people have it, and some people don't. I have it. You don't."

Dad had it because he worked at it his entire life. He also knew better than most how hard and cruel the game could be.

Born in Savannah, Georgia, in 1916, a place and a time when strict social structures shaped the young and old alike, Dad was raised a courtly southern gentleman. Savannah had rebounded after the Civil War quicker than other southern cities because of the port access it provided much of the eastern United States. It also maintained many of the rigid mores of the Old South. John Calvin had preached at the town's first Methodist church at the center of one of the city's antebellum squares, and his puritan code continued to dictate behavior at every level. In the nineteen-twenties, Savannah men still stopped walking and tipped their hats to passing ladies who, themselves, never ventured outdoors without headwear and dresses; young girls were thrown balls when they made their social debuts; and young boys like my father studied piano and sang in glee clubs. Elite women drank tea on Tuesdays and Thursdays, and every house of means had a drawing room with brandy, Cognac, and fine cigars.

My father was born privileged. His father, Eugene Harmon, had gobbled up farmland in Georgia and Florida for tract housing. When the American troops, the "Doughboys" came home after World War I, my grandfather offered them affordable housing and a fresh start on life. He and my grandmother, Willa, became affluent socialites in Savannah, and they joined the Savannah Golf Club, the second-oldest golf course in America. It was founded in 1794. I don't know if they joined because of my dad or simply because belonging to a golf club was what well-heeled Savannah residents did in those days, but neither of my grandparents played golf. In fact, the only member of their immediate family who took an interest in the game was my father.

Young Claude not only showed an interest, he displayed an amazing aptitude at an early age. Stories still circulate about my father's playing prowess as a boy—stories that have certainly been embellished, as I haven't found a living soul who saw him play in Georgia. Still, he must have shown some skill. When my grandparents moved to Orlando in the twenties, where Eugene owned most of the land surrounding what is now Dr. Philips Drive, The Bay Hill Club, Sand Lake, and Universal Studios, they joined two golf clubs so my father could continue to play. With cuffed sleeves, cotton knickers, and a dandy tie and touring cap, Dad walked the central Florida fairways swinging a hickory-shafted mashie from the A.J. Spalding & Brothers company and dreaming of playing the game like Francis Ouimet, Ted Ray, Harry Vardon, Walter Hagen, or that other young golfer from Georgia who was just coming into his own, Bobby Jones. At thirteen years of age in 1929, he had wowed the central Florida golf faithful by shooting an improbable round of sixty-three in an exhibition with Walter Hagen and Gene Sarazen. He also won the Florida high school championship and the national championship of club champions as a teenager. I can only imagine how his skills and dreams might have played out if the Depression hadn't hit.

No one in my family knows for sure how my grandfather lost it all in the crash of 1929. It's likely that he, like most real estate speculators, woke up one morning to find his stocks worthless and the banks that held his cash and mortgages padlocked shut. Tenants couldn't pay rent, so many simply loaded their belongings and slipped away. Tax liens came due, banks foreclosed, and by the time Bobby Jones, my father's boyhood idol, captured the final leg of his famous Grand Slam, my grandfather was broke. My father found himself at the doors of the Dubsdread Golf Club, hat in hand, applying for a job as a caddy.

"The game doesn't know who you are," Dad said for years, never once referencing his upbringing. "That ball and club don't know your name, and there's no room for a résumé on the scoreboard. There's space for a name, and there are boxes just big enough for numbers. If the numbers aren't low enough, nobody's going to ask how you did it, and nobody's going to care who you are. You don't get extra credit because your name is Harmon or Hogan or anything else. The game doesn't care."

When it came to golf, Dad treated everyone the same because

he knew the game would do the same. It was the great equalizer. In one of the first lessons I ever saw him give to the King of Morocco, he offered a variation of the same speech he'd given Billy on the range the day my brother didn't like the "feel" of his new grip. His Majesty took a few tenuous practice swings with a crowd of security guards, diplomats, ambassadors, and aides nearby. Everybody was nervous. Dad finally said, "Now, Your Majesty, before we get started I want you to know one thing: that ball and that club don't know that you're the King of Morocco. All these people know, but that ball and club don't know and don't care. The only way that ball is going to go anywhere is for that club to move it. The only way for the club to hit it is for you to swing it properly, no matter who you are." The King appreciated Dad's candor, and they became lifelong friends.

Whether you had everything or nothing, whether you had come from privilege and fallen into poverty or come from nothing and risen to greatness, the game treated you the same, and so did my father. When Dave Marr was a skinny nineteen-year-old kid from the oilfield plains of Texas, Dad hired him as a $250-a-month assistant pro who lived in an apartment over the locker room. That didn't stop Dad from inviting Dave down to Seminole, the famous Palm Beach golf club built by E. F. Hutton and designed by Donald Ross where Dad spent his winters. Dave stayed with our family just as any friend of Dad's would, regardless of his name or station in life. Many years later, Dave told the story of going to lunch at the Seminole clubhouse with Dad one afternoon. "It was a table of twelve, and Claude was the center of attention," Dave said. "He told one golf story after another and had everybody spellbound. After lunch, I said, 'Claude, who was that eating with us?' He said, 'That fellow on your left was Henry

Ford. The guy next to him was the Duke of Windsor, and the fellow on my right was Marshall Field.'" They were all the same in Dad's eyes. Good, bad, serious, or novice, they were all golfers.

Dad must have done an adequate job caddying as a kid. One summer he saved $86, a mighty sum for a Depression-era boy, and he couldn't wait to get home and present the cash to his father. My grandfather smiled, patted Dad on the head, and said, "I appreciate the sentiment, son, but you keep that money. We need a heck of a lot more than eighty-six dollars."

Because he had proved himself as a player, the members at Dubsdread treated Dad with a great deal of respect, offering him the best caddying jobs and putting him with the best players who visited the club. Any pro who came to town got my father as his caddy.

One of those pros was Ky Laffoon, a gregarious part-Cherokee tour player known for his hot temper and tart tongue. Laffoon, nicknamed "Chief," was the first player in tour history to have a yearly scoring average below seventy. He won a fair number of tournaments, too, but his temper kept him from becoming truly great. After one particularly bad putting round he strapped his putter to the back of his yellow Cadillac and dragged it down Route 66, sparks flying in its wake. As the story goes, he also carried a shotgun in his bag when he played the winter tour in Florida, ostensibly to shoot snakes, panthers, and other critters of the rural South. When his temper got the best of him, Chief's playing partners usually hid behind the nearest tree in case he went after other prey. Fortunately, he only ever injured himself on the golf course, and only then with his putter, which he fondly

called "my son-of-a-bitch." It didn't take many missed putts before Chief would slam the putter against his foot or throw it in
the air and let it come down on top of his head. Once, he hit himself in the face with the head of the putter after missing a short
one. When he regained consciousness and wiped the blood off
his head, his group was in the middle of the next fairway.

Chief liked Dad and used him as a caddy whenever he was in
town. When Dad was seventeen, Chief offered him a job as his assistant pro in Detroit. The salary was $30 a week, and he could
live in the bag room. It was an offer my father couldn't refuse. He
gave lessons in the summer, and in the winter, he and Chief
would close the shop and head to Florida where Dad lived hand-
to-mouth and shared $2 boarding rooms with his fellow pros on
the winter tour. He couldn't have been happier.

His next big break came in January of 1941 when he was
twenty-five years old. Still working for Chief Laffoon in the sum-
mers, Dad had become well known as a teacher, primarily because
of his good demeanor and ability to put almost any student at
ease. From the outset, Dad had a gift for making people relax.
He'd spend the first five to ten minutes of every lesson chatting
with his student about family, friends, and business. There were a
couple of reasons for this. First, he was genuinely interested. He
loved learning about people, and he had a fondness for hearing
what was happening in their lives. But also, he wanted his students
to relax and feel comfortable before trying to make a golf swing.

One of those early students Dad put at ease was Fred Corcoran, who would become one of the world's first sports agents,
representing Sam Snead and Ted Williams among others. At the
time, Fred ran the PGA winter tour, a string of events running
from January to early April in places ranging from Los Angeles to

Havana, Cuba, to Thomasville, Georgia. Most northern pros who could play at all tried their hands at the winter tour with the ultimate prize, the event that capped the "winter season," being the Invitational Tournament at Augusta National, better known as the Masters.

Dad wasn't thinking about the Masters in 1941. He was trying to make enough money in the Havana Open and the Miami Fourball to carry him through until springtime. That's where Fred Corcoran came in. Fred thought Dad was a wonderful teacher with a bright future, so he said, "Claude, there's an opening for an assistant's job at Winged Foot. I think you would be perfect."

Winged Foot was one of the most prestigious golf clubs in America, an extension of the New York Athletic Club with thirty-six of the best holes of golf anywhere in the world and a membership that was a who's who of New York's best and brightest. Bob Jones had won the 1929 U.S. Open there, and Tommy Armour, the legendary "Silver Scot," was a member. As assistant jobs went, there weren't many better. The only problem was, the head pro was Craig Wood, a world-class player who was about to win the Masters and U.S. Open himself. And Craig Wood didn't know Claude Harmon.

So Fred orchestrated a little subterfuge. He rigged the pairings at the next winter tour event, putting my dad in the same group with Craig Wood for what would turn out to be a four-hour playing interview. Dad, of course, was very nervous. On the first hole, Craig, who was strikingly handsome (think Michael Douglas in the movie *Wall Street*), boomed a drive that faded into the middle of the first fairway. Dad, who had never intentionally faded a ball in his life, hooked his tee shot into the left trees, chipped out, and made a bogey.

The second hole wasn't much better. Craig Wood, a long hitter in his day, drilled his ball down the middle, and Dad, fighting the hook, blocked his tee shot into the right rough behind a huge tree. From there his options were to hit a five-yard fade or a fifty-yard hook around the tree. That choice was easy: he couldn't fade the ball, so he took out a four-iron and hit a high, hard, hook that curved fifty yards. The ball landed just over a bunker and shot back toward the flag. When Dad marched out of the rough, he saw that his ball was four feet from the hole.

He was proud of himself until he heard Craig's comment. "Claude," he said, "that's the worst shot I've ever seen in my life, but I admire your imagination. When you get to Winged Foot, I'll teach you how to play golf."

Such was Dad's job offer.

That first summer at Winged Foot, Dad's boss won the Masters and U.S. Open championships. Had World War II not intervened, Craig Wood could have become one of the greatest players of all time and one of the most marketable athletes of his era. He had a breezy personality and the kind of chiseled features that excited advertisers. After his two major wins, Craig posed for a few print ads for Munsingwear and Pabst Blue Ribbon Beer, but timing did not work in his favor. His game peaked a little too early to take advantage of America's postwar golf boom. Still, he had the best club pro job in the country at Winged Foot.

When Dad showed up for work, Craig gave him very few options when it came to changing his game. "You can't compete against the best hitting that hook," Craig said. "And you'll always hit a hook if you continue playing with that grip." Dad had what we refer to today as a four-knuckler—a grip where the left hand was so far on top of the golf club that you could look down on it and see four knuckles. Mr. Wood insisted that Dad weaken his left hand (moving it to the left) to keep the clubface squarer on the takeaway. "If I see you hook another ball while you're working for me, I'm going to kick you in the tail," Mr. Wood told him.

So, Dad spent the summer of 1941 without hitting a single solid golf shot. This was particularly tough because it was his first season as the new assistant at Winged Foot—he wanted to make a good first impression on the members—and his boss was winning the two biggest tournaments in golf. Meanwhile, Dad was getting his hat handed to him by modest amateurs who couldn't win a club championship. It was a hard time, but Dad believed what Craig told him. The changes were necessary if he was ever going to be a great player.

It took a year for the new grip to feel comfortable—a long time for a good player to struggle with his game. During that same period, Mr. Wood had gone from a well-known club pro to a two-time major champion and A-list celebrity. He did print ads for Barbasol and Munsingwear, and signed endorsement deals with Forstner sport belts and Krementz jewelry for men. If World War II hadn't interrupted his reign, Craig Wood might have been the Arnold Palmer of his era. It took a lot of discipline for Dad to stick with the changes and hit it sideways, especially while his boss was reaching the pinnacle of the sport. But my father knew that golf was tough, and he knew that if he worked long and hard enough, one day the changes would pay off.

The process was tough. There was no "Eureka!" moment when Dad "got it." In fact, there were many months when he didn't know if he would ever get better. But slowly things started to turn around: he hit better shots and began to shoot better scores.

In the subsequent years, three people contributed to my father's success as a player and a teacher. The first two were Craig Wood and Ben Hogan. Craig had taught Dad how to swing the golf club. Mr. Hogan taught him how to play.

During World War II, Dad moved to Detroit to work in a munitions factory (he was unable to serve in the military owing to deafness in his right ear), but after the war, he returned to Winged Foot as the head professional. He was also hired as the head pro at Seminole Golf Club in Palm Beach in the winter. It was there that Dad became close friends with Mr. Hogan, who wintered in Florida and played most of his pre-spring golf at Seminole. They had known each other from the winter tours (Hogan used to bum car rides with Ky Laffoon), but it wasn't until Dad landed the Seminole job that they began playing a lot of golf together.

Dad learned the strategy of the game from watching Mr. Hogan. In their standard game, where missing a fairway or a green cost $10, Dad would hit driver on short par fours so that he would have wedge shots into the greens while Mr. Hogan would hit four-woods and eight-irons onto the putting surface. After a couple of days of watching Mr. Hogan play one hole this way, Dad said, "Ben, why do you hit four-wood off of this tee? There's no trouble up there, and you can get within a pitch shot of the green with a driver."

Mr. Hogan said, "I hit four-wood because you can't hit the fairway with driver, and I can hit the green with an eight-iron. I've already won forty dollars from you on this one tee shot this week."

That's when Dad began to learn how to play golf.

The third person who had the most profound influence on my father's game also had the most influence on his life off the course. She was the sister-in-law of the pro at Quaker Ridge, another classic course right across the street from Winged Foot. Her name was Alice McKee.

Mom lived in Boston, and before they were married Dad would catch the Sunday night train to visit her. When he straggled back into the golf shop late on Tuesday mornings, he would tell Craig Wood, "Sorry I'm late, I missed the train."

Craig would say, "I know you did, Claude. They only run every hour on the hour. Which one did you miss?" Finally, Craig said, "Claude, you're going to have to marry Alice. I don't give you enough time off for you to be running back and forth to Boston like this."

Dad became a much more accomplished player after he married my mother. She grounded him and kept him focused. Plus, once he had a family to support, he concentrated on his professional career. It was one thing to play for caddy fees and drinking money; it was something else to play for rent and groceries for two. He had always had a magical short game, learning to get the ball in the hole from almost anywhere. This was a great asset when he was hooking the ball because his shots ended up in some awful places. Once he stopped hitting a hook, his scores began to tumble. He could still get it in the hole from anywhere, but by hitting more fairways and greens he was making putts for birdies instead of scrambling to save pars.

By 1948, seven years after Craig Wood changed Dad's grip and saved his game, my father was recognized as one of the best ball-strikers in the game. Had there been a world golf ranking at the time, he would have been consistently among the top ten to fifteen players in the game. He had made it to the semifinals of the PGA Championship in 1945 before losing to Byron Nelson, and in the summer of 1947 he had fired a twelve-under-par sixty at Seminole, a record that still stands to this day despite advances in equipment, strength, fitness, and teaching, as well as turf conditions of the golf course. He had also won the Westchester Open twice and the Metropolitan PGA. Still, he went to the 1948 Masters as a "club pro" who was given little or no chance of winning. The only people who thought he had a chance were my mother and Mr. Hogan. Mom's confidence was based on faith; Mr. Hogan's came from experience. He'd played with Dad all winter. He knew what Claude Harmon was capable of doing.

Dad shot two-under in the opening round, a score nobody noticed. Lloyd Mangrum led with a sixty-nine, and Mr. Hogan, Herman Keiser, and Ed Furgol tied Dad at seventy. What the scores didn't show, and what no newspaper report picked up on at the time, was that the momentum of the tournament turned Dad's way in the heart of Amen Corner that first afternoon. After playing the first twelve holes in two over par, Dad hit his tee shot at the par-five thirteenth into some hard ground where the grass was thin on the right side of the fairway. With Rae's Creek staring him in the face, Dad had a tough choice to make: he could lay up short of the water and try to get up and down for birdie with a pin that was on the front of the green, the toughest play imaginable; or he could go for it. If he hit the green in two, he would certainly make a birdie and maybe make an eagle. If he missed the green and the ball ended up in the pond, he would probably shoot seventy-five or higher and be all but out of the tournament.

"It's time to separate the men from the boys," Dad told his caddy as he reached for his four-wood. He set up to the shot and remembered the thousands of shots he had hit in practice, preparing for this moment. He made the best swing of the week, and the ball flew perfectly. It landed on the green over the flag and rolled twenty feet away from the hole. A few minutes later, Dad rolled in the putt for eagle. Just like that he went from two over par to even par for the tournament. But more important, executing that shot under those conditions gave Dad a huge boost of confidence. He went to the fourteenth tee believing he could win the Masters.

He made another birdie at the par-five fifteenth when he hit the same four-wood into the center of the green on his second shot and two-putted for a four. Then at the tough par-four seventeenth he rolled in a twenty-footer for birdie and closed with a two-putt par in eighteen to turn what could have been a disastrous round into a one-shot-out-of-the-lead seventy.

He shot another seventy on Friday—two birdies and sixteen pars. Going into the weekend, Dad trailed Harry Todd by a single shot. On Saturday, paired with Dutch Harrison, a slow-talking, slow-walking pro from Arkansas, Dad had a great day on the greens and shot a three-under sixty-nine, to take a two-shot lead. After tapping in a par putt on the eighteenth that afternoon, Dutch took off his hat, shook Dad's hand, and said, "Mister Claude, I sure didn't know you could play that good."

Dad grinned and said, "Mister Dutch, I didn't do anything I haven't been doing all winter—just driving it straight and putting well."

"You sure did that, Mister Claude," Dutch said as they walked up the hill to the scoring table to sign their cards.

That afternoon reporters asked Mr. Hogan, who was the pre-tournament favorite in every tournament he entered and the leading money winner on the winter tour at that time, if he was surprised that a club pro like my dad was leading the Masters. Mr. Hogan said, "Absolutely not. I've played all winter with Claude and he's beaten me as often as I've beaten him. It would be a mistake to underestimate Claude Harmon."

Sleeping on a Saturday-night lead is never an easy thing.

When you're a club pro and you're leading a renowned tour pro like Chick Harbert by two shots, and everybody in attendance assumes you're going to choke, it's even tougher. Dad went through his normal routine. He ate the same breakfast and got to the course a little early to hit some balls.

As was the tradition at that time, the leader on Sunday was paired with Byron Nelson. Before the round began, Mr. Hogan cornered Dad in the locker room and said, "Don't let Byron intimidate you. He's going to be colder out there than normal because he thinks if he can get into your head, you'll blow up."

Dad laughed and said, "Ben, I don't think I'll have any trouble with him being cold. I've played all winter with you."

Sure enough, Byron wasn't his normally jovial self when he and Dad teed off. In fact, the round was pretty quiet. Nelson might have thought Dad was cracking when he three-putted for bogey at the par-three fourth. But Dad got the shot back when he hit a six-iron to within an inch of the hole at the par-three sixth. Then Nelson rolled in a thirty-foot putt for birdie at the seventh and stared Dad down as he stood over his twenty-footer. When Dad made his putt for his second birdie in a row, Byron turned and walked off the green without saying a word.

That fired my father up, and he ripped a tee shot on the par-five eighth hole up the right center of the fairway. Then he hit another perfect four-wood shot that never left the flag. The ball stopped three feet from the hole. When Dad rolled that putt in for eagle, he had an eight-shot lead with ten holes to play.

Craig Wood came out and joined Dad's gallery at the turn. "Keep it going," Craig said.

Dad laughed and said, "Craig, if I lose this tournament, I'm getting into another business."

A few uneasy murmurs started circulating through the gallery when Dad hit his tee shot short on the par-three twelfth hole and the ball rolled back into Rae's Creek. Undaunted, Dad took off his right shoe, rolled up the legs of his trousers, waded into the creek, and blasted the ball onto the green, twelve feet from the hole. He two-putted for bogey and the lead moved to seven shots. He put his shoe back on, only to have to take it off again at the par-five thirteenth. His second shot landed just short of the green and bounded into the creek again. This time, the ball was completely submerged, but Dad took off his shoe, waded into the water, and blasted it out as he would a buried sand shot. The ball stopped fifteen feet beyond the flag, and he two-putted for par. He left Amen Corner with a seven-shot lead. One more birdie at fifteen and a bogey at the par-three sixteenth were followed by two pars, for a final round of seventy.

As he walked up the eighteenth fairway, Dad knew he had the tournament won. "There's no greater feeling in the world," he said. "All I had to do was keep breathing, and I had the tournament sewn up."

He kept breathing, hit the green in two, and two-putted for par and a five-shot win over Cary Middlecoff. Dad also equaled the tournament record of 279 set by Ralph Guldahl in 1939. When the final putt fell, he took off his hat, waved to the crowd, and broke into a smile that wouldn't leave his face for many months to come.

At the green jacket ceremony, Bob Jones, founder of Augusta National, who played in his final Masters the year my father won, told Dad, "Claude, you're going to have all the club pros in the country playing in tournaments." He also invited Dad to stay in one of the club's cabins an extra day and play a round on Monday with him, Clifford Roberts, and General Dwight Eisenhower. Dad couldn't have been more thrilled. He had grown up idolizing Jones and had even traveled to Atlanta when he was eight years old to meet Jones at the train station after the U.S. Open. To win Mr. Jones's tournament was the thrill of a lifetime.

It also placed Dad in the most elite fraternity in golf. He would not win another major, although he led the U.S. Open going into the final round on three separate occasions. He would, however, play great golf for another two decades, setting course records at both the West and East Courses at Winged Foot, at Quaker Ridge, Seminole, and Fisher's Island—records that still stand today. He would return to Augusta National every year his health would allow, where he would attend the past champions dinner and enjoy the company of friends.

He would also teach golf for the next four decades, making sure each of his students knew that the game was hard and there was no shortcut to success. "If it was easy, everybody would do it." And as he reminded all of the Harmons more often than we can remember, not everybody had a Masters green jacket.

CLAUDE'S PEARLS

- Improvement requires taking a long-term approach. Anyone who tells you there's a quick fix is selling you a bill of goods.

- Nobody can ever perfect his or her golf game. The best golfers in history have gone through stretches when they didn't hit a single solid shot. Champions keep grinding, and fight through those times.

- Enjoy the game when you play well—because it's not going to last forever.

- Golf doesn't care who you are or where you're from. The game is about posting numbers by your name. And if those numbers aren't very good, nobody is going to remember your name anyway.

"The Big Picture Is
a Bunch of Little Details"

My first real golf lesson came from Jackie Burke, a man who would later become one of the most noted and quoted pros in the country. He certainly had better things to do than give a lesson to a kid who still chased butterflies, but I must have been driving my Dad nuts.

I was hanging around the golf shop at Winged Foot, waggling the clubs on the rack, asking one question after another, and making a general nuisance of myself. Dad was generally patient with us, but even he had his breaking point. Finally he said, "Jackie, take little Butch out and watch him hit a few."

Jackie grumbled something that sounded like, "Christsake," as he led me outside toward the tenth tee of the West Course.

"Aren't we going to the driving range?" I was only eight at the time, but I was sharp enough to know we were heading in the wrong direction. The range at Winged Foot was on the opposite end of the clubhouse.

"I'll teach, you listen," Jackie said.

Even in those days you didn't argue with Jackie Burke. Today Burke stories are legendary. One day at Champions Club, the course he built in Houston with partner and fellow major champion Jimmy Demaret, Jackie was giving tour pro Billy Ray Brown a putting lesson. Jackie started the lesson by saying, "Okay, Billy Ray, roll a couple for me." Billy Ray proceeded to roll an eight-foot putt an inch right of the hole, and before he could hit a second putt Jackie rammed the butt of his hand into Billy Ray's forehead. Billy Ray staggered back, shook his head, and looked up in time to see Jackie pointing a finger in his face and yelling, "I want it to hurt when you miss a putt!"

Thank goodness I was a kid; at least he wouldn't hit me. We got to the edge of the tenth tee and I pulled out the only club I owned, a cut-down seven-wood. Jackie teed up a ball and I flailed away. I topped the first couple, and the balls rolled into the valley that separates the tenth and eleventh holes. It took a while for me to get one off the ground, but I remember listening intently to what Jackie had to say. When I finally made solid contact, I held my finish in a pose that must have lasted ten seconds. Jackie just teed up another ball and said, "Okay, do that again."

The keys he hammered home that day were grip, alignment, and balance—the three most crucial fundamentals in the swing and about the only things you could teach a kid my age. I must have heard those words a thousand times over the next several years from my dad. Grip. Alignment. Balance. Grip. Alignment. Balance. Grip. Alignment. Balance. For a while I thought this was all there was to golf.

Years later I asked Jackie: "Why'd we go to the tenth tee instead of the driving range for that first lesson?"

He laughed and said, "Hell, you couldn't get it airborne. I

figured if I got you up on a hill, you at least had a chance of getting one off the ground."

When I finally got my father to go to the range with me, I was surprised by how little he said and how similar the things he did say were to what Jackie had already told me. "Your grip is the only contact you have with the club. If it isn't right, the rest of the swing won't matter," he said. "Get your hands on it properly, and you'll be ahead of the game." Then he talked about alignment, and finally balance.

Before the lesson was over, I said to him, "Dad, these are the things Jackie told me last time."

"They're the things I'll be telling you as long as you play," he said. And he did. For as long as I played golf and took lessons from my father, he always fell back on the fundamentals: grip, alignment, and balance. For a while I found this frustrating. I wanted Dad to tell me everything there was to know about the golf swing, and he went the other way, giving me advice in dribs and drabs, using as few words as possible, and often repeating the same themes over and over again. When I was young, I thought he was being intentionally stingy, that he knew the answer to the riddle but wouldn't share it. I wanted Dad to show me the "big picture," to give up the "secret" of golf to his son. There had to be a secret. (Mr. Hogan knew it and had promised to sell it to *Life* magazine!)

When I brought this subject up to Dad at the dinner table, he leaned back and laughed so loud the dishes shook. "There might be a secret hidden somewhere in *Life* magazine, but it's not the one you're looking for," he finally said. "Ben's secret is simple: he works ten times harder than everybody else and never stops learning."

Then Dad got serious. The smile faded and he leaned forward, putting his elbows on the table and lowering his head. "That secret you're looking for is fool's gold," he said. "There's no secret to golf, just like there's no one golf swing for every golfer. If there were one 'big picture' answer, everybody would know it. Truth is, that big picture you're looking for is nothing but a lot of little details."

At the time I didn't understand what Dad meant by that, and I didn't fully get it for many more years. It wasn't until I started caddying for my father during his afternoon rounds at Winged Foot that I slowly began to understand. Dad played a lot of golf with Tommy Armour and Craig Wood (who remained a member of the club long after he retired as the head professional), and when he did, I would be there walking every step. One afternoon when Mr. Armour struck a low, three-quarter six-iron shot that never left the flag and the ball hit short, jumped forward, and stopped a few inches behind the hole, I said, "Dad, how did he do that?"

Dad smiled and said, "Why don't you ask him?"

"Really?"

"How else you gonna learn?" he said.

So I nervously walked ahead and said, "Mr. Armour, if you don't mind my asking, how did you hit that shot?"

A huge smile crossed his face before he stopped, took out the six-iron, and explained that to hit a knockdown he focused on making a smaller swing, standing tall through impact, and keeping his hands passive. We stood there for five minutes as he explained every detail, including why he'd chosen that particular shot—"With the wind quartering in like this, you don't want to hit the ball hard and high, and with the pin cut on the back, you want to take the spin off so it will roll to the hole,"—and why having such a shot in his arsenal was so important—"A knockdown shot without much spin stays on line no matter what wind you're in." I was getting a seminar from one of the greatest players in history during the middle of his round.

From that point forward, Dad encouraged me to ask questions of everyone. When he played with Tommy Armour, Craig Wood, Sam Snead, Jimmy Demaret, Paul Runyan, Ralph Guldahl, or his assistants, Jackie Burke, Dick Mayer, Mike Souchak, or Dave Marr, I would carry Dad's bag and ask tons of questions: "Mr. Guldahl, how did you spin that wedge like that?" "Mike, how do you hit it so high with a one-iron?" "Mr. Armour, why do you work the ball against a crosswind?"

Starting at about age twelve, I began following my father during the majors as well. Mom traveled with him to the Masters, U.S. Open, and PGA Championship in the early years, but once the children started coming (Mom had six kids and ten pregnancies) she was tied up at home, so Dad and I traveled together. I would ask a thousand questions during the car ride and another thousand once we got to the course. During the practice rounds in the pre-gallery-rope days, I would walk the fairways with Dad, Mr. Hogan, and whomever else joined their group. I didn't ask as many questions during those rounds, but I still learned a lot by watching and listening. Dad and Mr. Hogan would dissect a golf course like skilled surgeons. Mr. Hogan used to play three balls in practice—one to the right side of the fairway, one to the left, and one in the middle. From there, he would play to various spots on the greens where he thought the tournament pins might be tucked. "Claude, I think when it's front right, you need to lay back near this mound," he would say to my dad. And Dad would answer, "You're right, Ben, and if they tuck it behind that left bunker, you want to be as far down the right side as possible."

I watched, listened, and learned. When we got back to our hotel room, I peppered Dad with more questions. For a player who was getting ready to compete in a major championship, he showed remarkable patience. If I had been in his shoes, I'm not sure I would have given the time or shown the care for a kid who asked questions by the bucketful.

What I didn't realize at the time was that I was learning the game, not through a book or a class or a seminar, or through Dad showing me the "secret"; I was learning by seeing, doing, and asking. I was piecing the puzzle together one tiny bit of information at a time, which was exactly what Dad had been saying. I was finding the big picture by learning the details.

Years later, I realized that this was the way my father and most of the players of his generation had learned the game. The first time I met legendary tour pro "Lighthorse" Harry Cooper, he told me, "Butch, when your father first came out on the winter tour as a teenager, I couldn't go to the hill [what most of the old pros called the practice tee] without him following me. I'd hit balls and he'd be right there behind me, watching. Finally, I got kind of aggravated and said, 'Claude, why do you watch me all the time?' He said, 'Because I've never seen anybody hit it that straight, and I want to know why.'"

Dad would watch anybody who could make him better, and he wasn't bashful about asking questions. Once when he and Mr. Hogan were practicing together, Dad asked a question about the swing plane. This was during a time when most good players were trying to swing more upright. Mr. Hogan gave Dad one of his devilish grins, pointed his thumb down the range at the other players, and said, "They keep trying to get their hands high, more upright, and I'm trying to get flatter all the time. As I get flat, when I move into the ball with my left side, it drops me inside even flatter and I come from the inside every time without ever coming over the ball. The flatter I get, the fatter my wallet gets." This wasn't a tip that would work for everyone (as Dad said, Mr. Hogan's only secret was his work ethic), but it was one more tidbit of knowledge my father added to his mind's database.

Dad got his weighted-driver idea from Gene Sarazen, who had gotten it from Ty Cobb. During a round at Augusta National, where Cobb (an Augusta native) was a member, Sarazen told the story of how he and Walter Hagen traveled to Great Britain by boat, and how they had a hard time adjusting because they couldn't practice during the trip. They hit balls off the deck into the ocean, but the rocking of the boat caused more problems than those practice sessions solved. So Cobb told him, "Ball players swing weighted bats before going to the plate. It makes their regular bats feel lighter, and they're able to swing with more power." The next week, Sarazen took the sole plate off a driver and filled the head with lead. The week after Sarazen shared that story, my Dad made his nine-pound driver, which he swung hundreds of times a day for years.

Dad approached learning golf the way an archaeologist approaches a dig. He would gather information from one source, test it, dig a little deeper, ask for additional opinions, then move to another area and dig a little more until he found something else. The thought of getting all his information from one source didn't make sense to him. He carried that same philosophy over to his teaching. He encouraged all his students to gather as much information as they could from as many sources as possible. If they wanted his opinions on what others were saying or doing, he would give it, but he would never say anything negative about another teacher.

When I was a teenager and playing competitive amateur golf in New York, I learned that one of the good amateurs in the region who had taken lessons from Dad for years had flown to Texas to take lessons from another well-known teaching pro. I was indignant. "Dad, can you believe Tom's taking lessons from that guy?"

Dad gave me a quizzical look and said, "What's wrong with that?"

"What's wrong with it?" I said, "He's disrespecting you."

His eyes flashed with anger. "No, he's not," he snapped. "He's trying to learn. That's what he should be doing. If somebody else can tell him something that will help him get better, he should listen. And so should you."

Dad insisted that my brothers and I seek advice from others, so much so that he sometimes set up rounds with his friends to help us with our games. When I was a teenager he announced one morning, "We're playing golf today with Johnny Revolta."

Revolta was the 1935 PGA Champion and a two-time Ryder Cup player. "Wow, Dad, that's great," I said. "Why?"

"Because he's the best wedge player I've ever seen, and you're the worst I've ever seen," he said. "If he can't help you, you're beyond help."

On the first hole, Revolta said, "Now, Butch, I can't tell you what I'm doing, but you can ask me anything you want."

As was the case with all of Dad's friends, Revolta answered every question and spent as much time as I wanted going through how and why he hit certain wedge shots. He would say, "Do you want me to hit a one-hopper or two-hopper?" and "Do you want me to skip and run this one in, or bounce and stop it?" There wasn't a single shot with a wedge that he couldn't hit, and not a single bit of advice that he kept to himself. Whatever I wanted to know, all I had to do was ask.

"You can take the guy who knows everything about the golf swing, but who has no personality or communications skills, and he'll give every member exactly one lesson," Dad said. "But the guy who knows half of everything but has great communications skills will be booked solid."

Dad knew that he couldn't communicate with everyone, and sometimes his best students couldn't understand a point he was making. When that was the case, he not only didn't mind when they sought the advice of others, he encouraged it.

Throughout my teaching career, but especially as I have become known for my work with top touring professionals, reporters have always asked me how I feel when one of my students works with someone else. I'm greeted with skepticism when I say, "Not only do I not mind, I think it's probably good." As my father never let any of his sons forget: no golf instructor and no single golfer has all the answers. The student who is truly interested in learning will gather information from a variety of sources.

I have had students take lessons from me, leave me to go with another instructor, come back to me a few months or a few years later, and leave again a few years after that. It's a natural part of the learning process. I believe that a good portion of my success as a teacher has been due to my acceptance of this fact of life and to my willingness to encourage people to listen to others—just as I did, and just as my father did when he was learning the game.

During the ten years we worked together, Tiger Woods solicited all kinds of advice from other players. Not only did I not mind, I encouraged it. Mark O'Meara, one of Tiger's best friends, gave him tons of advice while we were working together. Lots of other players helped him as well. I remember one week in 1999 when I saw Tiger on the putting green, gripping his putter so tight the veins were bulging on the back of his hands. "Are you trying to choke that putter to death?" I asked.

"What do you mean?"

"I mean, your grip pressure is about ten times what it should be. Relax your hands and you'll make a more consistent stroke."

When I saw little improvement, I came back to the putting green with a teaching aid, a small pad that attached to the grip of the putter. A sensor inside the pad measured grip pressure and a bell sounded whenever that pressure exceeded a certain amount. Tiger stood on the putting green for half an hour listening to that bell go off. He couldn't get his grip pressure light enough to stop it. Finally, he walked away. He needed to think about what we were doing.

Later, I found out that Tiger sought out Ben Crenshaw in the locker room at the Byron Nelson Classic. Ben is one of the best putters of all time. When Tiger asked him how much grip pressure he used with a putter, Ben said, "I hold it so lightly it almost falls out of my hands." After that, Tiger worked on lightening his grip pressure, and he shot 127 on the weekend and won the tournament.

Did I mind that my advice was being questioned? Absolutely not, because I knew what Tiger needed to do, but I also knew that he needed affirmation from one of the greatest putters of all time. Seeking that kind of advice is a good thing—something I encouraged Tiger to do when we were together and something I encourage all my students to do today.

I have always listened, watched, and read what others have to say. From the old pros like Jack Grout, who taught Jack Nicklaus the game, and the legendary Harvey Penick, to today's teachers like David Leadbetter, I try to soak up as much information as I can from as many different sources as possible. I've listened to the genius-who-was-ahead-of-his-time ranting of famous teacher Jimmy Ballard; I've spent time around Jack Lumpkin, who learned the art of teaching as an assistant at Winged Foot working for Dad; and I still enjoy watching the passionate delivery Bob Toski puts into every lesson he gives. David Leadbetter is one of the best communicators and one of the most studious golf instructors I've ever seen. He's also the man every teacher in America should thank for revolutionizing our profession. Prior to David, golf instruction was vaguely defined and teachers weren't paid very well. He turned that around through sheer tenacity and the strength of his personality. He also convinced the public that quality instruction was worth a premium price. Pros today have David to thank for at least half of their lesson income. Every opportunity I have to attend one of David's seminars I'm there, and I encourage my assistants to do the same. I don't always agree with him, but I know that whatever he says will be well thought out.

I've also read more golf instruction books than I care to count, starting with Mr. Hogan's *Five Lessons* and going through the most recent. When I hire a new assistant, the first requirement is that he or she read John Jacobs's book, *Practical Golf,* one of the best and easiest-to-understand golf books ever written.

I also encourage all my students, especially the young tour players, to watch the great players, ask questions, and do everything they tell them to do. When a young player is about to venture out onto the tour for the first time, I always say, "Okay, I want you to play a practice round with Tiger Woods as soon as you can, and ask him anything you want. Don't be afraid. He'll tell you whatever you want to know."

I did the same for Tiger when he was an amateur. I set up practice rounds for him and encouraged him to ask tons of questions of past champions. "Most of them want to help you because they remember what it was like to be where you are," I said, and he agreed.

When he was thinking about forgoing his final years of college to turn pro, for example, Tiger asked Arnold Palmer if they could have dinner together to talk about the pros and cons of that decision. Arnold was more than happy to tell Tiger about life on tour, especially as it related to the media and the other-than-golf aspects of being a professional athlete. Afterward, Arnold picked up the check for the meal, as he would under any circumstances, but especially for a college kid on a fast-food budget. Unfortunately, that violated NCAA rules. Even though Arnold wasn't encouraging Tiger to turn pro, or recommending that he choose a particular agent or play a particular brand of equipment, a professional athlete cannot pay for a college athlete's meal. Tiger had to send Arnold a check for his half of the bill. Arnold still has that check—uncashed—in his desk drawer. And while Tiger never said it out loud, I think that incident, and some of the other silly, nit-picking NCAA rules, pushed him to leave Stanford early and turn pro in 1996.

I encouraged Tiger to learn from others, especially people like Arnold Palmer and Jack Nicklaus, who had experience dealing with things Tiger would have to handle in his career. What I didn't do was encourage Tiger to stop working with me and seek advice from someone else; but contrary to what some might think, I wasn't angry or distraught when we parted ways, either. It's like Dad always said: "He's trying to learn. That's what he should be doing."

In late November 2004, I was launching the Harmon Tour, a mini-tour in the greater Las Vegas area that I started with a group of investors. We hoped to provide developmental opportunities for young professionals who weren't quite ready for the PGA Tour or the Nationwide Tour. As part of the marketing, I spent a lot of time doing media. One morning when I was at ESPN Zone doing radio and television interviews, the first question out of the box was, "So what's wrong with Tiger, and why do you think he refuses to come back to you?"

It was only the thousandth time I'd heard the question, and it was all I could do not to unclip my microphone and walk out. I was there to talk about the mini-tour, but after my breakup with Tiger, and after he failed to win a major in nine starts and lost the number-one ranking to Vijay Singh, I answered the "what's wrong with Tiger question" on an almost daily basis. My initial response was to yell, "If you want to know what's going on with Tiger, ask Tiger, or ask Hank Haney, his new instructor. I don't work with Tiger anymore. Stop asking!" But I didn't say any of those things. I said what I always said in answer to the question, which was, "Tiger is working on some swing changes, and I'm sure he'll get it together very soon. In the meantime, he's still got enough talent to win from the rough, so don't count him out."

This was my boilerplate answer because I believed it to be true. Tiger was and is talented enough and smart enough to win without his best stuff. He won two majors and six golf tournaments in 2005, and was two putts at Pinehurst away from another Triple Crown—a world-class season by any objective standards. He also regained his number-one ranking and won his seventh Player of the Year title. But even though the records continue to pile up, I see a different Tiger Woods today from the one I worked with in the late nineties and early in the new century. I'm not saying that he's better or worse now, or that the new Tiger is good or bad compared to the old one: he's just a different kind of player.

Today, I see a player who misses a lot more shots than he used to and who makes looser swings than he did five years ago. I also see a driven competitor who continues to win with different swings; I see a fierce competitor who is not afraid of any shot, any other player, or any condition; and I see a focused grinder who has developed one of the greatest short games in history. Tiger is also the greatest "trier" in the game. He is never afraid to try something different or learn something new. He thrives on knowledge and does what it takes to learn everything he can. He's a voracious reader, a great experimenter, and a person who relishes taking on new challenges.

I don't think he hits the quality shots he did in 1999, 2000, and 2001, but that doesn't mean he's not the best player. It just means he gets it done differently. Just look at his two major wins in 2005: He took a two-shot lead in the Masters by holing a highly improbable chip from behind the sixteenth green. Then he promptly blew his tee shot on seventeen dead right and made bogey. He made another bogey on eighteen when he pushed his approach into the greenside bunker, which allowed Chris DiMarco to tie him in regulation. Tiger birdied the first playoff hole and won the Masters, but the old Tiger would never have been in a playoff. He would have followed the birdie at sixteen with two perfect shots at seventeen and two perfect shots at eighteen. The field would have had to catch him. He would never have backed up to them.

At the Old Course in St. Andrews in 2005, Tiger overpowered the rest of the field by hitting the ball longer and putting better than everybody else in the field. But he also had two unplayable lies where errant tee shots wound up under gorse bushes, something that wouldn't have happened in 2000 and 2001. He still won. And nobody could deny he was the best player; he simply did it differently from years past.

That's what I believed when I was asked the question in 2004, and it's what I've continued to say today. Frank assessments are why Tiger and his father, Earl, hired me in 1992, and why they stuck with me for ten years. If anyone thought I was going to stop being pathologically honest in my analysis, they don't know me very well. Telling the truth in a no-nonsense style is why players seek me out. If I changed my style for one player, I would lose credibility with everyone else.

That blunt honesty created something of a mini firestorm at the U.S. Open in 2004, when I said Tiger wasn't swinging well and that in my opinion he was working on the wrong things, that his continual insistence that he was "close" was a form of denial. I made those comments in answer to a question on Sky Sports during a rain delay—part of a six-minute interview that covered a range of subjects. But when the "denial" statement hit the wires, I found myself in the hot seat. A reporter ran up to Tiger and said, "Butch says you're in denial. Do you have a comment?" That didn't make him happy, and I can't say that I blame him. He hadn't seen or heard the entire statement. All he'd heard was

"Butch says you're in denial." If I had been in his shoes, I would have been upset, too.

A week after the incident, I got a copy of the tape that included the entire six minutes, and I shot it off to Tiger with a note saying, "Here's the entire statement. You might not agree with all of it, but you should at least hear it in context." Not long afterward, he stopped me on the range and thanked me for the tape. He still didn't agree with everything I said, but he knew that I was being honest, just as I had been when the two of us worked together. He respected that in me then, and he appreciates it now. As far as the two of us were concerned, the incident was over.

Tiger and I are still friends. He phoned me with congratulations the evening after Adam Scott, another talented young player I coach, won The Players Championship, but Tiger and I don't spend a lot of time together. We speak when we see each other, but he's moved on and so have I. We're both fine with the time we had, and happy with where we are now. He's learning from other people, and that's great. If he wants to ask me any questions, he still has my number, just as I still have his.

Tiger paid me $50,000 a year. There was no exclusive—I always taught more than one player at a time—and there were no raises or bonuses, which was an unusual working arrangement for me in several respects. Today I don't charge any of my tour-player students. I'm the ultimate freelancer. I send the players I work with bills for my travel expenses based on how much time I spent with each of them, and I tell them that if they've had a good year, they can write me a check for what they feel I've been worth to them.

Other instructors tell me, "Butch, stop advertising that you don't have a rate or a contract with your guys. It makes it harder for us to put a price tag on what we do." Maybe, but I love the arrangement I have with my guys. The interesting thing is, the biggest check I've ever received came from the youngest player: Adam Scott. All my guys know that I don't work exclusively with anyone and I'm not in anyone's pocket. If you're one of my students I will be on the range all day, and I will eventually get to you. If that works for you, great; if it doesn't, there are plenty of quality instructors who would love to help you.

I can take that approach because of the quality people I work with, the relationships I have established in my years on tour, and the attitude I take to the lesson tee—one that I learned from my father. As long as a player is trying to learn, I believe in sharing what I know. If he can't get the answers he needs from me, I encourage him to go somewhere else and gather information from as many sources as possible. There is no "big picture" answer out there—or if there is, I don't have it. Learning is a long-term project for everyone, and there are a lot of people along the road who can give you directions if you're willing to listen and learn.

Sometimes I don't jump exactly when a player calls my name, but I always do my best to see everyone who wants to see me. When I first started working with Corey Pavin, for example, he called me during Bay Hill week and asked me to follow him during his practice round on Tuesday. I told him that I would, but when I got there, Adam Scott needed me, so I followed Adam. That afternoon, Corey said, "You didn't get out to me."

"I'm sorry," I said. "Adam needed me, but I'll get out tomorrow."

Wednesday, Freddy Couples showed up and needed me, and I didn't get out to Corey again. When I saw him on the putting green late that afternoon, he was a little irritated that I didn't make it out. So I told him, "Corey, there's a totem pole."

"Am I on the bottom?" he asked.

I said, "No, but you're not on the top."

The next morning, as he was on his way to the first tee for the opening round of the tournament, he walked past me, held up one hand, and said, "How, Big Chief."

That is the kind of relationship I have with my players these days, and it's the reason I continue to do what I do.

Tiger was a little different. I never charged him when he was a junior or a college player because I knew he didn't have much money, and what he did have he needed to save for travel and living expenses while he played tournaments. The deal I made with Earl Woods was that once Tiger turned pro, I would send them a bill and they could start paying me. We worked out a retainer in 1996, and our deal remained the same for seven years. At the end of the 2002 season, my contract wasn't renewed. I didn't ask. They didn't offer.

Some people have said that Tiger was unhappy about all the outside attention I was getting because of our relationship. I did become better known around the world because of my association with Tiger, but it was not as if I were invisible before. I had worked with Steve Elkington, Davis Love, and taken Greg Norman to number one in the world. I was already the only American golf broadcaster on Sky Sports, and I had plenty of world-class students.

People in golf knew Butch Harmon, but I'll be the first to admit I got a lot of added attention that I wouldn't have gotten had it not been for my association with Tiger. I also made a lot of money during that time. Neither Tiger nor anyone associated with Tiger ever said anything to me about endorsements or interviews, or the other clients I had (another common reason cited for our breakup).

I've always believed that Tiger simply wanted to hear new information, and he wasn't getting anything new from me. He always wanted something fresh, and he always wanted to learn. He was just like Tom, the member who I thought had two-timed Dad by going to someone else for a lesson; Tiger wanted something new and didn't believe that I was the guy to give it to him. There's nothing wrong with that. At the time, I believed that his swing wasn't broken, and it was a mistake to try to fix it. Tiger hit the ball better than anybody in the history of the game for two and a half years. I believed he needed periodic maintenance, not a complete overhaul. Tiger disagreed. But I'll never complain.

Most coaches go a lifetime without ever winning a championship. I saw two of my guys, Tiger Woods and Greg Norman, reach the top in one of the most difficult sports in the world. To recall another of Dad's great sayings, "Hey, life moves on. Enjoy the ride."

Learn everything you can from every person you meet. That's what I tell my students about golf, and it's what I tell my children about life. If any of my tour players see José Maria Olazábal practicing his short game, I tell them to stop whatever they're doing, watch him, and ask him questions. "He's the greatest guy in the world," I say. "He'll tell you whatever you want to know." Nick Faldo is the same way. Nick was one of the first modern tour players to take a video camera to the range and film swings. His video collection includes swings from Ben Hogan and Sam Snead to Ernie Els and Tiger Woods. The fact that Nick was the number-one player in the world when he was compiling this video didn't matter to him. He wanted to learn more, and he wasn't afraid to ask questions. Today, he's more than willing to help young players who have the same passion for knowledge.

A generation ago, this was the way things were done in professional golf. When Davis Love III came out on tour his rookie year, his father, Davis Jr., who was one of my dad's friends, called Tom Kite and asked Tom if he would mind playing a few practice rounds with Davis, answer his questions, and show him the ropes. Tom said that as long as Davis was out there to learn and be serious, he would help him any way he could. That was how things were done. Veterans took care of rookies. They showed them the ropes, answered their questions, and taught them the nuances of the professional game.

Davis and I have been friends since he first came out on tour, in part because our fathers were friends and came from similar backgrounds. Davis's dad was quite an accomplished player who had some good finishes in the PGA Championship, but Davis Jr. was best known for his teaching skills. He was one of the principal instructors for the Golf Digest Schools, a regular contributor to the magazine, and the author of many classic instruction books. He was also the director of instruction at the Sea Island Club in Georgia, an exclusive enclave between Dad's hometown of Savannah and Jacksonville, Florida.

Sadly, Davis Jr. was tragically killed when a chartered single-engine Piper Cherokee crashed in dense fog between Sea Island and Jacksonville. The entire Love family, including Davis III, who at the time was entering his third year on tour, struggled for a while. Grief is tough under any circumstances; when you're in the spotlight of the tour, and you lose a loved one in such a sudden and heart-wrenching manner, it's even harder. You can't disappear when you're a tour player. At times I know Davis wanted to vanish, just as I did when my mother passed away from cancer at an early age.

In 1990, not quite two full years after his father died, Davis and I were in Japan for a tournament. He was playing in the event and I was there on a semi-vacation with Jeff Sluman, who had worked with my brother Craig for years. Davis played poorly, barely making the cut. For an American tour player to barely make the cut in Japan he had to be hitting it sideways. That Friday night we all had dinner together, and Davis said, "Would you mind having a look at me? I'm hitting it terrible."

I said, "Sure, Davis, just give me a call when we get back to the States and I'll be happy to have a look."

"No," he said, "I mean now, in the morning."

I said, "Davis, it's the middle of a tournament."

But he said, "Yeah, and I couldn't play any worse than I'm playing."

I went out the next morning and saw that his shoulders were too steep, and he was far too active with his lower body. Davis is a tall guy, and tall people need to keep their footwork more passive than do short players. Also, I wanted him to level out his shoulders through impact to free up his arms. We worked on that, and on making contact with his sternum directly over the ball, something we call "covering" the shots. The results were positive. Davis shot 131 on the weekend and finished third in the tournament after almost missing the cut.

I also tried to help Davis develop, mature, and take a long-term approach to playing the tour. Like most outstanding athletes, Davis wanted to win every tournament and was unhappy when he went more than a couple of months without a victory. I explained to him that the PGA Tour was not like the NFL, where the average career lasts five years. A healthy tour player can remain competitive for thirty years—longer if he transitions to the Champions Tour. I told Davis what I tell all my players: one or two bad tournaments do not define a thirty-year career.

When Davis played in his first Ryder Cup matches in 1993 at the Belfry near Birmingham, England, I did very little teaching and spent most of my time trying to calm him down, which is what I assume his father would have done and what I know Dad would have done. Davis was paired with Tom Kite in the foursomes matches (which is the alternate shot segment). They had already decided that Davis would drive on the odd holes and Tom would drive on the even holes because of the way the course was designed, but Davis was as nervous as a cat. The thought of hitting the first tee shot of the matches petrified him. Throw in the fact that there was a fog delay, which prolonged the time he had to think about it, and Davis was a virtual wreck by the time play began.

"You're going to be fine," I kept telling him. "Just relax. You'll hit it great and do fine."

Then, as they were walking off the putting green toward the first tee with thousands of spectators lining both sides of the fairway and hanging over the grandstands between the first tee and eighteenth green, Davis turned to Tom and said, "Why don't you hit on the odd holes, and I'll take the even."

"What?" Tom said.

"You take the odd holes. I think I need to take the even holes," Davis said.

Tom put his arm around Davis and said, "This first hole is just a little three-wood off the tee. Don't worry about it; just make your swing and play your game. We've already decided that the odd holes work out better for you and the even holes are better for me, so let's just stick to the plan and have some fun out there."

Davis was so pumped up he must have hit that opening tee shot three hundred and twenty yards with a three-wood. He played great and has had an incredible Ryder Cup and President's Cup career ever since. Davis later admitted to being petrified. He was sure that if he played poorly in that first Ryder Cup he might never recover. I knew better, and so did Tom Kite. This was a lesson only experience would teach. I'm glad I got to help Davis learn it.

Davis now works with Jack Lumpkin, the director of instruction at Sea Island, so he is still getting Claude Harmon's pearls. (Jack was one of Dad's assistants.) Davis gets the benefit of learning from my father, even though he never met him. Come to think of it, a lot of people do.

I helped Davis at a time when he needed to hear what I had to say, just as Tom Kite helped by showing him the ropes on tour. When Davis got as much from me as he could use, he moved on to Jack Lumpkin; and Bob Rotella, the famous sports psychologist and author, helps him with his attitude and mental approach to the game. That is how it should be. Davis wants to learn; teachers like Jack and me want to teach; and veterans like Tom want to help young players preserve the professional game for future generations.

I hope that same sense of congeniality continues for generations to come. The fraternity of golfers demands as much. Plus, the intricacies of the game are too complex to be learned in one or two settings from a single source. Dad used to chastise my brothers and me during our teenage years by saying, "It's what you learn after you know it all that counts." His point was that you never know it all, and once you realize that fact, you can begin the learning process in earnest.

CLAUDE'S PEARLS

- There is no secret to golf, and no single source for everything you need to know.

- Listen to everybody. You'll always pick up something.

- If somebody tells you he's "got it," that he's figured out the game, play that person for everything he owns.

- Don't be afraid to ask questions. Great players were not always great. Most of them remember what it was like to struggle, and many of them are happy to help someone who is genuinely trying to get better.

- If you learn every little detail, pretty soon that big picture you were looking for starts to take shape right in front of you.

- It's not an insult when someone seeks advice from someone other than you. A person trying to learn will gather as much information as possible from many different sources.

- It's what you learn after you know it all that counts.

Three

"Don't Ever Mix Your Ego and Your Ignorance"

In 1931, at the ripe old age of fourteen, Dad qualified for the U.S. Amateur Championship at Beverly Country Club in Chicago. He and my grandfather took the train from Orlando. They got there early so Dad could get in a few practice rounds before the tournament, which was eventually won by Francis Ouimet (the same Francis Ouimet who, seventeen years earlier, defeated Harry Vardon in the U.S. Open).

When they arrived in Chicago, Dad walked out onto the tee. An older man was standing there. "Are you waiting for someone?" Dad asked.

"I am," the man said. "If you're alone, go ahead and play."

Dad took a few swings and hit a couple of balls from the first tee. Then the man said, "You know, I've waited long enough. If you don't mind, I'll join you."

"Don't mind at all," Dad said, and he introduced himself. He was always gregarious and outgoing, even as a teenager. Striking up a conversation with an older competitor was nothing out of the ordinary. Nor was it out of character when Dad said, "You want to get up a game?"

After a slight pause, the man said, "Sure, we'll play a little game."

Dad figured the guy had to be in his late fifties or sixties, so he said, "If you want, I'll give you a couple of shots a side."

The man said, "No, son, you keep those shots in your pocket. We'll play straight up."

Sixteen holes into their round, the man had closed Dad out of more money than he had brought for the trip. Fortunately, my grandfather meandered onto the course, and Dad discreetly borrowed enough cash to pay his debt.

As Dad shook the man's hand on the eighteenth green and reached into his pocket to retrieve the money he'd lost, the man, who turned out to be H. Chandler Egan, the winner of back-to-back U.S. Amateur titles in 1904 and 1905 and a famed course architect, said, "That's all right, son. Keep your money. But let this be a lesson to you. Don't ever mix your ego and your ignorance."

Thirty years later, my brother Billy won the New York State Boys Championship at Briar Hall. It was the first time Billy had seen Mom and Dad cry. When he asked them what was wrong, Dad said, "Nothing's wrong, son. We're crying because we're proud of you." He was proud of all of us, even though there were times in our lives when we didn't give him much to be proud of, but he rarely showed that kind of emotion. Only two other times do I know of my father weeping: one was at my mother's funeral and the other was the day Dave Marr won the PGA Championship.

Mom, Dad, and my brothers watched the tournament on our boxy black-and-white RCA television in the living room of our New Rochelle, New York, home (I was away in the Army). According to my brothers, when the final putt fell and Dave won, Mom and Dad put their hands over their faces and cried like children. Dad never talked about it, but Mom said later, "Dave is like a member of the family. Your father loves him like he loves you." We later found out that Dave's son was born that same afternoon, so Dad had a gold money clip made for him. On one side was the PGA of America logo and the date, August 15, 1965, and on the other side was a Saint Christopher medal with the notation, "Anthony James Marr, born August 15, 1965, What a Day!"

The year after Billy won his Boys Championship title, he traveled to Jamestown, New York, to defend it. Dad didn't make the trip, but Billy kept in touch by phone every night. When the pairings came out for the first match, Billy drew a local kid named Timmy Rocket. Billy knew him. Timmy hadn't finished within ten shots of Billy in any of the events they'd played together. So when Dad asked, "Who are you playing?" Billy said, "Dad, I've got the closest thing to a bye."

"Is that right," Dad said.

"Yeah," Billy continued. "I'm playing a kid named Timmy Rocket. He can't play dead."

The next morning, Timmy Rocket birdied three of his first four holes to put Billy in a three-down hole. My brother hyperventilated for the rest of the round, knowing his words from the night before were coming back to haunt him. He lost the match two-and-one, and my father never let him forget it. "Timmeeeeee Rocket!" Dad would shout. "Closest thing to a bye! Rocketed your butt right out of Jamestown, New York."

Billy would hang his head, but Dad would always follow the dig with the same tidbit of wisdom he'd learned from Chandler Egan: "Don't ever mix your ego and your ignorance, son."

None of us was immune from Dad's ego-deflating wit. When I was playing the tour (unsuccessfully) in the late sixties, I called home one Friday after missing my third cut in a row. Dad answered the phone, and I said, "Dad, I need to come home and see you. I'm just playing awful."

"What are you talking about?"

"Dad, I'm playing terrible. I just missed another cut, and I have to go to Canada to qualify on Monday. I need to come see you."

"You missed the cut?"

"Yes, I missed another cut."

"I thought you were leading," he said. "I must have had the newspaper upside down."

Dad never let us forget that anybody who was playing bad was only one round away from turning things around, and anybody who was playing good was one quarter-inch of ball position from playing terrible. It was only a matter of time before every golfer turned his game around, one way or the other. He also constantly reminded us that golf was a game in which anybody could beat anybody on any given day, so mixing your ego and your ignorance resulted in a toxic brew.

Whenever we were feeling good about ourselves and our games, he would walk out to the first tee with us at Winged Foot and say, "Okay, boys, when you swing at it sixty-one times I want you to stop, look around, and think about where you are on the course." Dad held the records on both the East and West Courses with scores of sixty-one. On the East Course he had been twelve-under through thirteen holes playing with woods that were actually made of wood and looked like pool cues compared to today's jumbo-headed titanium clubs; with irons that looked like butter knives; and with balata rubber balls that had all the pliability of a modern-day racquetball. Anytime we needed an ego check, he would remind us of those sixty-ones—and the sixty-one he'd shot across the street at Quaker Ridge, and the sixty at Seminole, and the sixty-three at Fisher's Island. He also never let us forget that only one member of the Harmon family had a green jacket. This was his way of reminding us not to mix our egos with our ignorance. The only person who could quash *his* ego was my mother, who would let him go on for a while before saying, "Claude, you won the Masters in forty-eight, but you haven't won it since," which always called him to smile sheepishly and pipe down.

Keeping your ego in check was one of Dad's most ardent lessons, one he had learned over and over again throughout his career. A lot of people ask me why Dad didn't play the tour full time. He certainly had the game for it. There were a lot of great full-time tour players who never won majors and who never came close to finishing as well as Dad did in the U.S. Open and the PGA Championship. On the few occasions I broached the subject with him, the answers were always short—usually one word: "Money." Years later, when he was giving an interview with a reporter for *PGA Magazine*, I heard him expand that answer for the first time.

"Being the pro at Winged Foot is quite an honor," he said, "and the tour was not what it is today. I remember shooting two under par in the Crosby one year and not making any money at all. The guy who shot three under par won seven dollars. In the

1955 U.S. Open at Olympic, I finished thirteenth and won $225, and for three consecutive years I finished in the top twenty in the Open and made a total of less than a thousand dollars. Remember, I was paying my own entry fees, hotel bills, travel expenses, and caddy fees. I ate at hospitality rooms and that sort of thing to defray some expenses. And remember, the golf courses on tour ranged from just okay to very poor in those days. The good clubs didn't want the tour taking away their courses for a week."

I had never heard him lay it out in those terms before. He avoided going into a lot of detail with us, in part, I believe, because he never wanted us to think that we were the reason he had forgone a playing career, even though we clearly were. Mom and the children needed a home, food, and something resembling a stable life. The tour offered none of those things. Ben Hogan's wife, for example, told friends that she and Mr. Hogan had decided that the tour and children did not mix, so they didn't have kids. As Sam Snead joked for years, "Those who were lucky made enough money playing the tour to survive, and those who were really lucky got club jobs and settled down."

Dad did very well in all his club jobs, in part because they were the most prestigious jobs a pro could have. Thunderbird in Palm Springs, which was the winter job he took after leaving Seminole, was the best club in the desert for many years, a place where Bob Hope, Bing Crosby, and Randolph Scott went to get away for the weekend. At Winged Foot, he owned the golf shop and kept five to six hundred bags in storage at $25 a bag. His lesson book was as full as he wanted it to be, and he continued to play in a fair number of local and national events that paid relatively well. One Pro-Member event in Piping Rock, New York, for example, had a winner's purse of $1500—more than the first-place check at a lot of tour events at the time. Dad won it more than once.

Plus, he had members who supported him. There was no Costco or Golf Warehouse selling golf clubs and golf balls when Dad was a pro. If you wanted a new driver, you went to your local pro and bought what he recommended, and you paid full retail. By the same token, the business practices of golf pros lacked the kind of retail savvy you find today. "Turn" was a term you applied to backswings, not inventory. Billing controls consisted of scraps of paper piled on the corner of Dad's desk, and "inventory creep" was the foul-mouthed drunk who counted boxes in the back room once a month.

To give you an idea of how business operated in those days, Tommy Armour, who remained a member at Winged Foot long after he retired from competitive golf, told Dad every year that he needed to order fifty sets of Tommy Armour Silver Scot irons and woods, twenty-five sets with stiff shafts and twenty-five sets with regular shafts. Then, throughout the year, as Mr. Armour would play with members, they would always ask, "Tommy, what clubs do you think I should play?"

He would put his arm around any member who asked and say, "Tell you what I'm going to do. I'll call the factory this afternoon and order a custom set of clubs that suit your game perfectly. Don't worry about a thing. I'll take care of it."

After the round, Tommy would stick his head in the door of Dad's office and say, "Claude, in two weeks stick a set of regulars in Mr. Smith's bag." Dad sold fifty sets of Tommy Armour Silver Scots every year based on Mr. Armour's "custom fitting" technique.

Those practices worked fine in the golf business—it was recreation and sport, after all, with the pro being the ultimate authority—

but as Dad painfully discovered, similar practices didn't fare so well in other industries.

In the ultimate mix of ego and ignorance, Dad and his former boss Craig Wood accepted a wonderful gift from one of Dad's Seminole members, a gift that would end up costing my father almost everything he owned. The member was Henry Ford, and the gift was a Ford dealership in New Rochelle, New York. Wood-Harmon Ford was launched with great fanfare not long after Dad won the Masters. Local papers covered the grand opening as if it were the first and only car dealership in the county. Dad and Mr. Wood were local celebrities—a fact everyone assumed would drive foot traffic to the showroom floor, and why wouldn't they? This was long before Nissan and Toyota were household names. A Ford dealership was a license to print money, especially in the boomtown fifties, when communities like Levittown were springing up throughout the Northeast and Americans were buying cars and other luxury items in record numbers.

A year into the operation Craig Wood wanted out, and Dad bought his interests. The new name on the door was Claude Harmon Ford. Dad hired a dealership manager, checked in periodically, and figured everything was rolling along smoothly. The manager seemed to know what he was doing. Dad had a shop manager to handle the retail operations at the clubs. Having a manager for the auto dealership was the same thing, or so he thought. Three years in, Dad learned the awful truth. The manager he had hired was a gambler and a thief. When Dad's accountants finally uncovered the problem, and Ford Commercial Credit called in the notes on his inventory, it was too late. The manager Dad had entrusted to run his dealership had embezzled $750,000. All the money was lost.

Dad had assumed that the force of his personality and the name recognition that came with being a Masters champion would be enough to make his dealership a success, even though he knew as much about owning a car dealership as Lee Iacocca knew about winning golf championships. He had mixed his ego and his ignorance with ruinous results.

By every definition of the word, we were bankrupt. All accepted rules of accounting gave Dad no option. He needed to file the paperwork, take his lumps, and walk away. There was no shame in being victimized by a crook; he should have declared bankruptcy and moved on with his life. But that was not how Dad thought. He had seen his father lose it all, but my grandfather hadn't walked away from his obligations. If my grandfather had survived the Great Depression with the Harmon name intact, Dad was not going to sully it over a car dealership. There were plenty of discussions in our house during that time—tense discussions between Mom and Dad that we were not invited to join—but the option of bankruptcy was not something either of them was willing to contemplate.

Golf pros are notoriously bad businessmen. If you look at annual bankruptcy statistics, club pros rank high on the list of professionals who file Chapters 7, 11, or 13 every year. Most get overextended in their golf shop inventory, buying clubs that won't sell or ordering twelve dozen sweaters when you couldn't find twelve people who would wear them. Ego and ignorance tend to run amok in our profession. But Dad never had any problem running the golf operations. His shops always showed a profit even though his controls and practices weren't models you would teach at business school. Venturing into an unknown arena is what got my father into trouble. To get out, he realized he had to stick to what he knew.

Dad did a very brave thing. He went to a dozen of his friends and asked for help. For a proud man, these were tough calls. He didn't want their money, although any one of them could have written a check for the complete amount. Dad was not about to accept charity, nor was he going to owe money directly to a member or a friend. All he wanted were co-signers on a bank note. He would pay off the debts himself. Every friend he asked agreed to sign the note.

It took Dad more than twenty years to pay everything he owed from that mistake. I never heard him complain or shift blame, and I never saw him lose his composure, although there were plenty of tense, lean years in our house during that time. I did hear him discussing the belt-tightening with my mom. One night they were discussing Billy's school, a very nice Catholic elementary and middle school near our home in New Rochelle. Mom thought the tuition was too expensive, but Dad said, "He's gone there his whole life. I can't ask him to graduate from another school because of something I did. We'll make it. I'll just have to figure out how."

And so, Dad taught more lessons, sold more equipment, and worked harder at squeezing everything he could out of a dollar. Throughout my life, I have heard and read stories from old touring pros who claim they were down to their last dollar when they finally played well enough to keep going. Mr. Hogan told stories about starting out on tour with a slush fund of $75. By Christmas of that year he was down to fifteen cents and had to eat oranges he picked from the trees that lined the fairways in California. If he didn't play well in those final weeks of December, he wouldn't have enough money to return to Texas. But he did play well, and the rest is history. Dad didn't have one of those stories because if playing golf had made his situation better, he wouldn't have had any problems. He could still compete with the greats of his day, but tournament purses weren't enough to pay what he owed.

Dad was never late on a bank payment, and his friends who co-signed the note were all sent copies of the cancellation notice the day he finally cleared the account. It was a great lesson for all of us, but not the lesson Dad thought. He would have certainly pointed to this episode as the ultimate example of mixing your ego and your ignorance. But we saw something different: we saw a man in insurmountable debt who clawed and scraped and dug himself out. We saw a man who could have, and probably should have, declared bankruptcy, but who refused to soil his family's name by even considering it. He might have looked in the mirror and seen a man who let his ego get the best of him. We looked at him and saw a man whose character we could only hope to emulate.

I can't tell you the number of times I've warned my students about mixing their egos and their ignorance. I've seen my fair share of young hotshots who have challenged Corey Pavin to various games because they could drive the ball a hundred yards longer than Corey. At the conclusion of those rounds, I make a point of finding those guys to rub it in.

Anybody can beat anybody in golf. Jack Fleck, a pro from Davenport, Iowa, denied Mr. Hogan a fifth U.S. Open title, and Rich Beem held off Tiger Woods to win the PGA Championship.

Who would have believed that with Davis Love, Ernie Els, Tiger Woods, and Thomas Bjorn vying to win the British Open at Royal St. George's, a rookie from Kent State named Ben Curtis would end up with his name engraved on the Claret Jug? The fact is that golf is a game where anything can happen. The moment you let your ego believe otherwise is the moment you're in for a rude awakening.

CLAUDE'S PEARLS

- In business, in golf, and in life, ego and ignorance are a lethal combination.

- When you think you're playing the next best thing to a bye, you're as good as beat before the round begins.

- Anything can happen in golf. Anybody can beat anybody on any given day. If that weren't the case, there'd be no reason to play.

- If you're playing well, just be patient; it won't be long before you can't hit it in a forty-acre field. And if you're playing bad, keep working; you're not far from playing good again.

- In the end, all you have is your name and your reputation. Don't soil either.

"Sometimes the Easy Answer Is the Right One"

I remember asking my father once, "What's the most important position in the golf swing?"

He looked at me like I'd grown a second head. "Impact," he said. "Nothing else matters. The ball's only on the club for a fraction of a second. After that, you've got no control over it. What else is there?"

That was the kind of no-nonsense answer and matter-of-fact approach that made Dad so popular. He gave straightforward advice and didn't expound when no explanation was necessary. I remember when one of his students, a good player, asked him about the "lower lateral shift and how it relates to the exterior rotary vector." Dad laughed and said, "I assume you're talking about weight shift, but I can't be sure, so let's start with the clubface and your hands and work back from there."

This was typical Dad. He didn't believe in complicating the uncomplicated. If you could fix a problem by making one simple correction, why not do it? Of course, you had to know what the problem was and what one simple correction to make, which was another of Dad's gifts. He could always find the one thing in a swing that would correct ten problems, not ten things the student needed to do to correct one problem.

A lot of people can look at a player and give a boilerplate explanation for why shots move one way or another—"You're hitting it low and left because the clubface is closed at impact," "You don't generate any clubhead speed because you have a reverse pivot"—that sort of thing. But there is artistry in knowing how the fundamentals of the swing apply to each individual athlete and to mentally cataloging every swing you've seen.

Dad had total recall when it came to golf. He could watch a player once, and not only have the swing and the putting stroke seared into his memory but also use that player's actions as an example to help others. "You remember all those putts Jack Nicklaus made when it counted?" he said. "He did it because of his stance. He crouches so low that his right forearm is parallel to the ground, and his right wrist is cocked as far as it can be. That forces him to use the bottom muscles of his right forearm, the ones around the ulna bone that are not twisters. Using those muscles allows him to putt with his right arm like a piston." This was not something many people saw, but Dad was convinced this was Jack's putting secret.

He had similar theories about other players. He thought Sam Snead swayed during his swing because he was so flexible in his hips and legs that he needed the additional motion to provide a solid base to release the club, and he believed that minimal wrist cock made Tom Kite both a relatively short driver and one of the best wedge players in the world.

None of this was formulaic, though Dad treated each golfer and each golf swing as unique. None of my brothers teaches the same way, either, just as none of us have the same personalities. We are individuals, and we treat our students as individuals. The only constants in any of our teachings are the fundamentals: grip, posture, stance, balance, and alignment—the keys that were hammered home to us by our father.

A lot of people who attend our seminars are surprised when Craig and I disagree on a subject or a method, but it happens a lot. We don't consider it odd at all. Craig's students think he's the best in the business, and my students stay with me because they think I know what I'm doing as well. There's nothing wrong with either of us because in golf, there is no one way to teach.

The one thing we Harmons do alike is this: we keep our messages simple. None of us looks for a complicated answer when a simple one will suffice, and we all have unwavering confidence in our beliefs when it comes to golf, just as our father did. Dad was not one of those instructors who said, "Well, you know, maybe you should try something like this," or "I think you might be doing that." Dad would say, "Here's what you're doing, and here's what you need to do to get better." No hesitation, no ambiguity, no games, and no BS—that's the only real Harmon method. If you want an instructor who will soft-pedal his analysis, don't come to us. And if you're looking for validation for your own beliefs, we're not for you, either. Dad never said, "What do you think you're doing?" and when you gave some nonsensical answer, say, "That's amazing! I'm seeing the same thing." Dad believed that his job as an instructor was to teach, and the student's job was to learn. If you wanted head nodding and hand licking, you should buy a dog. If you wanted to improve your golf game, you should hire someone who studies the game passionately, who wouldn't hesitate to teach, and who has a proven track record of success. Dad had all of those things. Through time, his sons developed the same traits.

I wish I had been so gifted in my early years. As a young professional just getting started, I walked out to the range to give a lesson to one of our older members. "What's the problem?" I asked.

"Shanks," he said.

"Oh?"

"Every shot."

"Well, let's have a look."

And for the next twenty minutes, he shanked every shot. I did everything I could. I talked to him about setup and weight transfer, about spine angle, and about the role of the arms in relation to the shoulders and torso. We talked about wrist cock, hinge, lag, and the position of the chin at impact. And he still shanked every shot. A half hour into the lesson I decided I couldn't charge the guy. I couldn't help him! I also knew I needed help if I was ever going to survive to teach another day. So I went into the shop and said, "Dad, I need your help. My lesson's got the shanks and I've got no idea what to do."

He could have quietly walked out to the tee to help me, but that wouldn't have been Dad. "Sooooo, Butchie's got a shanker and can't get him squared up, huh?" he shouted so loud that everyone in the shop and a few people in the locker room could hear. "Need me to come bail you out, huh?"

"Dad, could you just help the guy. He's about to quit, and so am I."

Dad laughed the entire way to the driving range. When he got there, he watched my student take one swing, and said, "To stop shanking, you've got to understand what causes a shank in the first place. Most people assume that the clubface is open and that the hands are in front of the ball. They think this causes you to make contact where the clubface meets the hosel. In fact, the opposite is true. A shank is caused by a closed clubface. You release the club early, throwing it at the ball on the way down. This shuts the clubface and traps the ball between the hosel and the ground, causing it to shoot to the right—a shank. Because people think they've got the clubface open, they work hard to close it, which only exacerbates the problem. The more closed you try to get it, the more likely you are to hit a shank."

Then Dad held the club and guided my student through several half-swings, taking the club back hip-high, and through hip-high keeping the clubface square and maintaining the angle of his left arm and wrist through impact. Five minutes later, the guy was hitting it right down the middle.

"How'd you do that?" I said. "You only watched the guy shank one shot, and you knew exactly what he was doing."

"No, I knew what he was doing before I stood up from behind my desk," Dad said. "The ball tells you everything you need to know. A shank is a shank. I knew the guy was hitting it with a shut clubface before I walked out here. The only question left was, what did I need to tell him to get him to stop?"

"I didn't know you shanked it because of a closed clubface," I said.

"That's because you've never had to figure it out for yourself to keep from starving to death," he said.

Dad was right. Unlike many of the players from his generation, I had never had to dig the game out of the dirt for myself. I had always had the best teachers and the best equipment, been around the best players, and had access to the best books and magazines. I had never been a thousand miles from home with a hundred dollars left to my name and a cruel case of the shanks. Dad had, and he had worked on the problem until he figured out the answer.

He also knew that every golf swing was as unique as a snowflake, and every student learned the game differently. Keeping things simple was the only way to teach such an individual sport. As he told *PGA Magazine* in the early seventies, "I learned very early that you have to teach golfers as individuals. Sure, golf magazines might tell you that the same theory applies to all, but that's a joke. Golfers come in all sizes, shapes, and reflexes. That's what you start with. Then you have to fit them to a swing and a game. When I go to the lesson tee with a member for the first time, I've only got a minute or two to size up the pluses and minuses of what I've got to work with and where we have to start. Some things are easy, because you can't learn trigonometry if you don't know algebra. A lot depends on the individual. How much time and inclination does he have to practice? How athletic is he? What other sports has he played? These are all factors."

Dad viewed the tendency of golfers to overanalyze and overcomplicate things as a neurosis. "Look, it doesn't have to be complicated," he used to say. "You can't reinvent the wheel. Fundamentals are still fundamentals. Good players are still good players. Good golf swings are still good golf swings. Good putting is still good putting. And the easy answer is still the right one most of the time. Just look at the record books. You'll see that there are a lot of different ways to get there."

He had no time for those who thought you could teach or

learn cookie-cutter golf. When one amateur showed up and said, "Claude, I want you to teach me to swing like Sam Snead," Dad said, "Okay, let's go to the putting green."

The guy said, "No, I don't want to putt like Snead. I want to swing like him."

But Dad insisted that they go to the putting green. When they got there, Dad dropped a ball into one of the holes, and said to the student, "Can you pick that ball out of that hole without bending your knees?"

The guy looked into the hole and said, "No."

Dad said, "Well, Sam Snead can, so let's forget about what he does and start working on what you can do."

Another time in the late sixties, a member from Bel-Air Country Club had flown in to take a lesson from Dad. The guy was a California big shot. We knew this because he arrived in a limo, his long hair looked like it had been styled on the way in, and he wore more gold than Deion Sanders. If we missed all those things, he told everybody he met what a hotshot he was. He personified all the things Dad despised. In addition to that, he had a huge golf bag with his name embroidered on the side. Dad knew every good amateur in the country. His philosophy was, if you were good enough to have your name on your bag, he should know who you were. He didn't know this guy.

To make matters worse, the fellow spent the first five minutes of the lesson telling Dad how to teach him. This was during the time when Jack Nicklaus was winning every tournament in sight, and much was being made of Jack's lower-body strength. The guy had convinced himself, as had a lot of other people at the time, that all the power in the golf swing came from the legs. He wanted my father to teach him how to use his lower body more effectively.

The one thing you didn't do was tell my father how to teach. But Dad kept his cool. He told the student that the legs played an important role in the swing, but that they were only one component.

The guy wouldn't have it. He not only insisted that all the power in the swing came from the legs but he also demanded that Dad teach him how to use his lower body to gain more yardage. After a few minutes, Dad had heard enough. He teed up a ball, took out a driver, knelt down on his knees, and hit it two hundred and fifty yards down the range. Then he stood up, handed the driver to the student, and said, "Why don't you stick that club up your rear end and see if you can hit it that far by swiveling your legs."

That was the only time I ever heard my father be that curt with a student, but he'd had enough of this poseur. He also had no use for gimmicks and what he termed "trendy teaching." Despite his own innovations—film projectors, weighted clubs, shaft extensions to keep the hands out in front of the ball through impact—he was not a big proponent of radical theories and what's-hot-today techniques. I remember a time when a lot of instructors were having students hit balls with beach balls between their knees to promote leg separation through impact. When I asked Dad what he thought about it, he shook his head and said, "That was invented by somebody who never had to post a score by his name."

"So, you don't think knee separation is important?" I asked.

"That's not what I said."

"Well?"

"Look, if you're standing on the eighteenth at Pebble Beach needing a par to win, you better not be thinking about a beach ball," he said, the finger working overtime as he punched each word.

"The Pacific Ocean's on your left. You want a beach ball, just hook your tee shot down there and you can have all the beach balls you want. If you want to win the golf tournament, you better have the heel of the club coming down ahead of the toe, because if that toe comes in first, you're not winning."

Simple, but that was how Dad viewed the game. If a pro worried about knee separation, or what the club looked like at the top of the backswing, or his foot action through impact, Dad wanted to play that person. "The game's not called 'pretty,' it's called 'golf,'" he would say. "And in golf, how you do it doesn't matter. The scorecard doesn't tell anybody if you holed a fifty-foot putt, or hit a two-iron to two feet. All it shows is the number of shots you took."

Having played with most of the great players in the modern era, my father believed that today's teachers would have screwed up players like Byron Nelson, Raymond Floyd, and Lee Trevino. He believed that Nelson didn't know that he dipped and swayed through impact, and he wouldn't have been able to play if someone had told him to stop. Likewise, any pro who had gotten hold of Lee Trevino as a kid would have told him there was no way he could play taking the club so far outside the line and rerouting it at the top the way he did. Ray Floyd jerked the club inside the line and got it so flat on the way down that it looked like a baseball rather than a golf swing. Any good modern teaching pro would have made young Raymond correct that move. Ben Hogan swung very flat and cupped his left wrist so that the clubface remained open throughout the downswing. No instructor would teach that move today, and many would have told Mr. Hogan that he had no chance of playing well if he didn't work on a more upright plane. Yet all of those guys played pretty well.

"You can work with nature, but you can't change it," Dad said. "Don't ever change what a person does naturally." He didn't live to see them, but I'm sure he would have said the same thing about players like Sergio Garcia, Jim Furyk, and Paula Creamer—all great players who have unorthodox moves.

He also had a saying that sums up the way his sons now teach the game. "If you believe in what you're doing, don't be bashful about saying so, forcefully. If you don't believe what you're doing, don't say anything. A halfhearted opinion's worse than no opinion at all."

I have had the good fortune of coaching many of the best players in the world, and I'm constantly asked what the "Harmon method" is for teaching. That answer is no different today than it was when my father was teaching forty years ago. I believe, as he believed, that you work with what a player does naturally; keep things as simple as possible; and never back away from what you believe. That is how I have been able to successfully work with players of different builds, differing abilities, with vastly different swings who have wildly different egos. If there were a Harmon Method or a Harmon Swing, then Adam Scott's swing would look like Corey Pavin's, who would look like Stewart Cink, who would swing like young LPGA star Natalie Gulbis. The fact is that none of the players I work with swings the club alike because none of them is built the same and none of them has the same natural gifts.

I laugh these days when people accuse me of having the secret of length. Granted, I coached Greg Norman, who was one of the longest drivers of the golf ball in his prime, and Davis Love, who was the longest in the game until John Daly and Tiger Woods came along, and of course Tiger, who is as long as anybody who ever played. But all of those players hit the ball farther before they started working with me. I shortened them up so they could find the fairway.

I also followed my father's advice, working with nature instead of fighting it. Perhaps the greatest example of this came when I was approached about working with Natalie Gulbis. Before I ever stood on the range with Natalie, I had several friends call me and say, "You don't want to work with this girl. That swing is way too strange. You don't want to have your name attached to that kind of move."

"No," I said. "I'm going to work with her if she wants because I want to see how someone makes contact with that kind of motion."

At the top of her backswing, Natalie's head is turned a hundred and eighty degrees away from the target, and the club is pointing ninety degrees to the right of where she wants the ball to go. Her backswing looks like a left-handed player's follow-through. Then she drops her head six inches on the downswing. When I first saw her, I said, "How do you swing with that big dip?"

She said, "What big dip?"

That's when I knew I had to work with her. A player with enough eye-hand coordination and natural ability to hit the ball well with that kind of unorthodox swing was someone I could help. I also wanted to see if I could work with what Natalie did naturally. I could have told her to revamp her entire swing; I could have tried to make it more classic, or "prettier," as Dad would have said in a not-so-kind way, but that would have been the worst thing an instructor could have done for Natalie. While I would never teach Natalie's swing to a beginner, it works for her, and I work with what she does naturally.

Natalie is a fantastic talent, a great person, and a dedicated player, which is another reason I wanted to work with her. She is wrongly called the Anna Kournikova of golf because she's very attractive, and as of this writing, she hasn't won yet. But that will change. Natalie is driven to win and won't be satisfied until she has many victories. When we began working together she fully expected me to recommend a revamp of her golf swing, and she was a little surprised when I didn't. "You're not going to tell me to change the position of the club at the top?" she asked.

"Why would I?" I said. "You don't hit the ball at the top of the backswing. Impact's the only thing that matters. Let's work on that."

We worked nonstop on limiting the amount that her spine angle changed and her head dropped during the downswing, and we made sure that her shoulders were aligned to deliver the clubhead on a path toward the target. Then we made sure her lower body continued moving and her hips cleared through impact. This was important because if her hips were slow, the club tended to move down instead of out. (That produced some low and left shots.)

I had Dad to thank, again. He taught me to always shoot straight, and Natalie appreciated my honesty and the no-nonsense style. I had some definite opinions about Natalie's swing (although they weren't the ones she expected) and I shared them, forcefully, just as I do with all my students. Not only did she take my advice to heart, she incorporated an aggressive strength and fitness program into her daily routine.

For Natalie, the work we did together coupled with her own

natural talent and drive paid off in late 2005, when she was a stalwart on the victorious U.S. Solheim Cup team. With a 3–1–0 match-play record against Europe's best players, she proved herself a champion, even though she doesn't have the shelf full of trophies yet to prove it.

People also have some misconceptions about the work I do with Adam Scott. Because Adam's swing looks so much like the swing Tiger Woods had in 1999, 2000, and 2001, people assume that I taught Adam to swing like Tiger. Nothing could be further from the truth. When he first showed up at the University of Nevada–Las Vegas, I saw him take one swing and said, "Whoa, I've seen that move before." He came to me with the swing he has, and I worked with what he did naturally. It just so happens that Adam's natural swing looks a lot like the swing Tiger had when he was the most dominant player in history. It won't be long before Adam breaks out and becomes a dominating player in his own right.

But few people I've taught have moved me, and few provide a better example of my dad's adage that you have to "believe in what you're doing, and say so forcefully," than Fred Couples. Freddy came to me as one of the most down-and-out players I'd ever seen. His back had been giving him problems for years, his game was all but gone, and he was contemplating retirement at the ripe old age of forty-four. It was a mighty fall for a guy who spent his entire career being loved by everyone. Women loved him because they thought he was sexy. Kids loved him because they saw Freddy as an overgrown kid, a goof-off who could quote lines from the most recent episode of *South Park*. Men loved him because he was the epitome of cool. He was both Fred and

Freddy. The fact that his life and his golf game had gone through such major upheaval made me relate to Fred unlike any other player I worked with. I think I connected with him because I too had struggled as a player. While I never achieved the kind of success Fred had on the golf course—he and my dad shared one major victory, the Masters—I had questioned my abilities in the three years I played the tour, and I often wondered what the hell I was doing. Fred had all of those same feelings and many more.

We also shared similar personal stories. Fred had lost his father, and he had gone through an ugly divorce that made headlines in the Palm Beach papers. While my divorce from my first wife hadn't been fodder for the society pages, it was no less painful. By 2002, both Fred and I had finally found peace. He had settled down and was content with his life, and I had finally found happiness with my wife, Christy, a woman I had first met when she worked for me as a shop girl in Bettendorf, Iowa. We rekindled our relationship years later, and by 2001 we were married and now working hard at raising our son, Cole. I felt a kinship with Freddy, so when he approached me in a state of depression over his golf game, I said, "Come on, it can't be that bad."

"No, it is," he said. "I can't hit a shot."

"You always say you can't hit a shot," I said. "You're always whining."

Ten minutes later on the driving range, I said, "Wow, you're right, you can't hit a shot."

Freddy had gotten himself into such a bad position that he couldn't hit two nine-irons in a row on anything resembling the same line. He had the club so far underneath and inside that he had no consistent ball flight or direction, a situation that would have been bad with a driver, but with a nine-iron it was disastrous.

"Okay," I said, "I want you to aim way out to the right and come over the top to pull it on line."

He tried, failed, and hit the ball dead right.

"Jeez, that's terrible," he said.

"You're right," I said. "Do it again, only this time, come over it and pull it on line."

Again he tried, and failed.

"Just come over it and pull it," I said.

We stood out there for four hours. He hit at least five hundred shots with a nine-iron and by one o'clock in the afternoon he still hadn't come over one and pulled it. We broke for lunch, and then spent another three hours on the range. I knew we had to break down Freddy's habit of getting the club underneath and flipping it with his hands at impact. I knew he was a gifted, coordinated athlete who still had game, but he had a lot of work ahead if he wanted to mount a comeback.

If I was going to help Freddy, I knew I had to have a heart-to-heart with him about commitment and desire. I'd learned from Dad that there are some guys you need to hug and some you need to kick in the rear; some you need to make laugh and some you need to make so angry you think they're going to cry. What I needed Freddy to do was tell me he had the desire to put in the work it would take to succeed. In a similar situation my dad would have given me a verbal kick in the rear. I was the type of person who responded to that sort of motivation. So was Freddy.

"Nobody would look down on you if you walked away right now," I said to him during our come-to-terms conversation. "You've had a great career, and you have a great life. You've made a lot of money, won a major, won a lot of golf tournaments, and have a lot of fans. You can go up in the television booth and be an analyst, or become a course architect, or go into the club or clothing business and nobody will blame you. In fact, most people will support you. I happen to think you've got a lot of golf left in you, but that's up to you. If you're serious about making these changes, you're going to have to work harder than you've ever worked in your life. Right now, you don't act like you want to play."

"I'm ready," he said.

And he was. The time and effort Fred Couples put into his game made me proud to know him.

He always made a huge shoulder turn, worked his arms inside and underneath, and flipped the club with his hands at impact, but he's so athletic and has such great eye-hand coordination that he's able to get away with a swing that I would never teach to any beginner. I worked with that swing, leaving what Freddy did naturally but getting him to change his address position, setting up with a more closed stance and with most of his weight preset on his left side. This allowed him to continue making the large turn, but also got him in a position to cover the ball more at impact. We spent many hours working on these changes, and he spent even more time perfecting the new move.

That effort paid off in April 2003, when Fred won the Houston Open, his first tour victory in five years. That Sunday, I was in Iowa attending my mother-in-law's funeral. It had been an emotional week for my family, just as it was for Fred. When Christy and I got back to our hotel after the memorial service and wake, we turned on the television in time to see Freddy's postvictory interview. He got out one answer, but then he broke down and wept, covering his face with his visor before walking away.

"Wow, I never expected that," the CBS Sports announcer Jim Nantz said. Nantz should have known: he and Fred were roommates at the University of Houston and had been best friends for two decades. That said, I never expected it, either. Freddy astounded all of us, not just with his comeback but also with the passion with which he did it. I've never been prouder of a student in my life. And I've never gotten more joy out of a victory.

But the highlight of Fred's mid-forties career came in September 2005, when Jack Nicklaus picked him to play on the President's Cup team. A lot of people think Fred doesn't care about a lot because of his laidback attitude. Fred is a guy who doesn't answer his phone because he thinks somebody might be on the other end. Not only will he not answer, he never checks his messages, either. The only way I can reach him is to call his caddy, Joe LaCava, and have Joe hand him the phone. But when it comes to team competitions, Freddy becomes deadly serious. Anytime he discusses the Ryder Cup, he gets animated and, in some cases, angry. He's sick of the United States teams getting beat, and he hopes to someday be a Ryder Cup captain so he can put an end to the losing streak.

When Fred was named to the President's Cup team a week shy of his forty-sixth birthday, he felt as though he had been given new life. On the Sunday of those matches, with the Americans and Internationals tied going into the singles matches, Fred went to Captain Nicklaus and said, "I want Vijay Singh." At the time, Vijay was the number-two golfer in the world, having just lost the number one spot in the world rankings to Tiger Woods.

Just as he had done in 1992 and again in 1994 in the President's Cup, Fred holed a birdie putt on the eighteenth hole to win his match, this time against the International team's top player. In those previous two appearances, his winning putt at eighteen won the cup for the U.S. team. In 2005, he secured the seventeenth point, assuring at least a tie. The United States went on to win by a score of 18½ to 15½.

When I saw that putt go in, I knew that I had been right about Fred Couples. He still had a lot of golf left in him, and a lot more heart than anyone could imagine.

The simple answer had been the right one for Freddy. All he needed was someone to show him the way, believe in him, and occasionally kick him in the rear. I was happy that I could be the one to fulfill all those requirements.

All you need to do is look at the golf games of my students like Freddy, Ben Crane, or Darren Clarke to realize that there are thousands of ways of getting the club square and moving along the target line at impact. My job is to identify a player's strengths, or as Dad said, "size up the pluses and minuses of what I've got to work with" and maximize those strengths without corrupting what the player does naturally.

Because of my belief in my Dad's adage that golf is not called "pretty" for a reason, I am the only instructor on tour who does not carry a video camera to tournaments. For starters, I think the camera has become a crutch. Anyone can film a swing and tell you why you don't look like Tiger Woods. I wonder what today's video experts would have said if they'd been asked to analyze Ben Hogan's flat, slashing action fifty years ago or Lee Trevino's loopy cut swing in the seventies. Those players learned to let the ball be the barometer of their successes. I believe in doing the same. I also avoid showing video to my tour players during tournament weeks because I know they would find plenty of things wrong with their swings if they watched themselves. You won't find a more self-critical group of people than tour players. Like the golfer standing on the eighteenth at Pebble Beach, I don't want my guys worried about a beach ball between their legs or how pretty their swings look at the top.

My brother Craig once asked Dad what it would take for him to play like Ben Hogan. Dad put his hand on Craig's shoulder, laughed, and said, "Son, you can't make a racehorse out of a mule. What we can do is make you the world's fastest mule." This was his way of telling Craig not to worry about playing like Mr. Hogan: not only could Craig Harmon not do it, nobody else in the world could emulate Mr. Hogan, either. It is always best to work with the gifts you have, even if it means accepting that you can only be the world's fastest mule.

A lot of things I see and hear on tour make me think of my father, and his insistence on keeping things simple and being straightforward in sharing what you know. One morning in South Africa his spirit was more present than ever. It was the President's Cup, and the morning fourball matches were about to go out. Captain Jack Nicklaus had paired a couple of veterans—Jay Haas and Jim Furyk—against a couple of young guns—Adam Scott and Stuart Appleby. Adam, as I've said, is a student of mine and Stuart is a great guy and friend, but Jay and Jim are also friends and fellow Americans, so my allegiances were torn. Plus, my brother Billy was Jay's caddy—had been for years—and it was hard to pull against family.

Billy was standing on the range with Jay as the four players warmed up. He had seen all four of them hit so many golf shots over the years that he didn't think much about the differences in their moves. But that was not the case for many of the fans in attendance that day. It was Jim's first visit to South Africa and the first time many of the fans had ever seen Furyk and Haas up close. The murmurs were palpable. Adam and Stuart had classic golf swings, the kinds that make great magazine foldouts. Jim's and Jay's swings had more loops than a calf-roping contest. As they walked off the range toward the first tee, Jay said to Jim, "I bet those people in the bleachers don't give us much of a chance."

Jim laughed, and they proceeded to thump Adam and Stuart six and five.

As Dad always said, there's no place for style points on the scoreboard.

Most of the players I work with ask questions about my father, even though some of them never met him and most never saw him hit a shot. Stewart Cink and Justin Leonard are great fans of Dad's and fantastic students of mine. I think of all the players I work with today, Stewart and Justin are the two who have made the most visible changes in their golf swings since coming to work with me. Stewart is a tall man who used to have a narrow, handsy swing. Now he gets a lot more turn and width in his swing. Justin used to set up on his left side, collapse his arms at the top, and use his hands throughout the swing, hitting the ball low and occasionally left. Now he sets up with his spine angle tilted to the right, and he gets a lot of arm separation at the top of his backswing. Darren Clarke is one of my favorites, primarily because he reminds me so much of my father. Always smiling, joking, smoking his cigars on the course, and buying a round of Guinness in the clubhouse, Darren is what Mr. Hogan had in mind when he called my dad a "jolly golfer." He loves fast cars, fine watches, and a good joke, which makes him more like Claude Harmon than any other player I work with.

In the WGC Match Play Championship in 2000, he and his good friend Tiger Woods ate breakfast together and were joking before their final match. Tiger was heavily favored, although I knew it was going to be a good match, as Darren is a great player who was hitting the ball very well. At breakfast that morning, Darren said, "If you hole a long snake and give one of those run-across-the-green fist pumps, I'm coming after you with a big Irish fist of my own."

Tiger never missed a beat. "Give it your best shot," he said. "You're so fat, you couldn't catch me."

We were all laughing so hard we had to wait a few minutes to compose ourselves before leaving the locker room. A few minutes later, as we were all on the range together, Darren was on the left side of the range and I was standing with Tiger on the right. It was the first time I'd ever had two students playing together in a match-play final, so I was as nervous as the players. I was assured of having one of my students win, but I was also assured of having one lose. Darren sensed the tension and lightened the mood on the range by shouting out, "Don't worry about me, Butch. I'm hitting it fine. You stay down there and mess him up." The gallery erupted in laughter. Everybody loved it, just as they love Darren everywhere he goes.

Later that afternoon during the lunch break, Tiger decided to hit some practice balls between the morning and afternoon rounds. When I asked Darren if he wanted to go to the range as well, he said, "Are you kidding? I'm not walking all the way down there. Go wear Tiger out. I'm going out on the porch to smoke a cigar."

That's why Darren is the most popular European player in

America, and why I think of him often. He's a down-to-earth person, a great guy, and a wonderful player—someone who, in my estimation, will be winning tournaments and making friends for
many years to come.

And by the way, Darren beat Tiger that afternoon to win the
WGC Match Play.

CLAUDE'S PEARLS

- There's one position in the golf swing that matters: impact. Everything else is window dressing.

- If the answer seems simple, that's probably because it is. Don't overcomplicate it.

- If someone tells you that there is one "perfect" golf swing, walk away and don't listen to another word he says.

- You can't make a racehorse out of a mule, but you can become the world's fastest mule.

- If you believe in what you're doing, say so loudly and proudly. If you don't, keep your mouth shut because a halfhearted opinion is worse than no opinion at all.

"If You Aim at Nothing,
You're Always Going to Hit It"

I was hitting balls on the range in the California desert one sunny morning when my father rode out in a cart, stood behind me, and crossed his arms in silent observation. I was swinging well, which was always a plus when Dad was around. After a couple of minutes, I wanted him to voice some validation for the hard work I'd put in. But he just stood there, arms folded across his giant chest, not uttering a sound. Finally, I said, "What do you think, Dad?"

Without hesitating, he said, "I think if you're aiming at the mountains you're hitting it great."

Mountains surrounded the golf course on all sides.

This was another of Dad's witty but poignant ways of pounding home a point he made often: if you aim at nothing, you're always going to hit it. He would often say to me, "If you don't have a target, you're wasting your time. Golf is not about great swings, or hitting the ball solid on the clubface, or hitting the driver three hundred yards. When you strip the game to its basics, it is about advancing the ball from point A to point B. If you are standing at point A and don't have a point B in mind, you might as well be hitting it with a baseball bat."

Dad believed that any work that was not target-oriented was not only wasted but also destructive, because you were conditioning your mind to think about the wrong things. Many times he told my brothers and me, "You're just swinging away and hoping the world moves underneath you. You might as well take up tennis."

As far as he was concerned there were four types of golfers. First, there were those who are "ball oriented," who don't think of anything other than hitting the ball. You've certainly seen those kinds of players. They're the ones who glance at the target one time and spend the rest of their pre-shot routine staring at the ball and tensing to hit it. Rarely are they very successful.

The second kind of golfer, according to Dad, is one who is "swing oriented." The ball and the target are secondary; they just want to make good swings. They might look at the target for a second or two, and look at the ball during their swings, but their minds are on the mechanics. You've seen these guys as well. They are the ones who go through a mental checklist during their pre-shot routine—"left arm straight, spine tilted back, hips tilted up, chin high, eyes on the ball . . . now Swing!" Swing-oriented players might hit solid golf shots, but they can't play golf. They are what we call "Ranger Ricks," guys who can hit it well on the range when they don't have to chase their errant shots, but on the golf course they don't know how to score.

The third kind of golfer is the one who doesn't think about anything other than getting it over with. This is the guy who is so self-conscious about his lack of skill that he blanks out and hits every shot as quickly as he can, as fast as possible. His only thoughts are turning the spotlight on somebody else.

Finally, the fourth kind (in Dad's view, the only true golfer) is the "target-oriented" player, the one who spends all his time thinking about where he wants the ball to go. This is the player who picks a line and spends 95 percent of his pre-shot routine focusing on that target. He visualizes the trajectory and curve of every shot, and imagines how the ball will react once it hits the ground. He senses wind direction and the thickness of the air, and he factors in those things as he plots how he's going to get the ball to his target. He only thinks about the ball as it relates to the lie and how that lie will affect ball flight. And he only thinks about the swing as it relates to the type of shot he wants to hit. Every synapse of his brain is geared toward hitting a specific shot to a specific target. As far as Dad was concerned, target-oriented golfers are golfers. The rest are jolly strollers—recreational players who can enjoy the game but who won't get much better.

The question Dad asked every student before he swung was, "What's your target?" If the student said, "I don't have one; I was just trying to swing," then Dad would spend the entire lesson trying to turn the student into a target-oriented golfer. The mechanics of the swing could wait. He knew that if he couldn't change the orientation, nothing else mattered. "Major trophies are full of names of guys with unconventional swings," he said. "But a guy who doesn't focus on his target won't win a two-dollar nassau."

Dad believed that the great golfer honed in on as small a target as possible and forgot everything else. I remember playing Winged Foot West with him once, and when we came to eighteen, I asked him how he planned to play his approach. I was being a bit of a smart-ass. The pin was cut just over the crest of a severe false front. Any ball short of flag high would roll forty yards back into the fairway. I was giving Dad a hard time about the difficulty of the shot he had.

He didn't notice. "I'm going to cut it onto that mound three feet short and six feet left of the hole," he said.

"What mound?"

"The one I'm about to hit," he said. And he hit a perfect iron shot that started at the left fringe and faded toward the hole. It hit a couple of yards left of the flag and funneled down, stopping three feet behind the hole. When I got to the green, I saw that the mound Dad was aiming for was nothing more than a knob the size of a kindergartner's desktop. It was, indeed, two yards left and one yard short of flag high. His ball mark was right on top of it.

If my brothers and I ever hit a shot without a specific target in mind, Dad would never let us hear the end of it. When Billy played in the Palm Springs Invitational as a junior, Dad followed him, as he did when any of us where playing. The first hole was a straightforward par-four with a road (out of bounds) on the right. It was a simple driver and wedge hole, the kind of clear-your-throat opener that lets players ease into their rounds. Billy hit a good drive, but on his second shot, he let the out-of-bounds stakes on the right creep into his mind. Of course, he pulled the ball into the left greenside bunker. For his third shot—a simple bunker shot—he looked up during his waggle and all he could see were white OB stakes, the road, Our Lady of Solitude Catholic Church on the other side of the street, and Dad, arms folded across his chest, standing directly on his sightline twenty yards away.

Billy had no chance. Instead of blasting the ball onto the green, he caught it cleanly, and it soared out of bounds, directly toward the church. Billy hung his head, knowing that he was about to make a seven on this simple par-four. Then he heard a voice. It was Dad, shouting, "Light a couple of candles for me while you're over there!"

Had Billy been a little older, he might have given Dad the finger. That night he said, "Dad, I didn't appreciate the comment you made on number one today. It was disrespectful during what I consider a very big tournament."

Dad said, "Don't blame me. You hit that ball exactly where you were looking. I knew you were heading for the church before you pulled the trigger, so I figured you could light a couple of candles and maybe say a few 'Our Fathers' for me while you were there."

Billy gritted his teeth and didn't say anything. He knew Dad was right. He had hit his approach shot into the bunker because he had focused on where *not* to hit it rather than on the target he wanted to find. He then hit the sand shot exactly where his eyes fell, the only place he couldn't hit it and make a decent score on the hole.

"You had ten thousand square feet of sand in that bunker," Dad said. "And you hit the ball—the only thing you couldn't do—because all you saw were those big white out-of-bounds stakes."

Dad believed that focusing on the wrong target was just as bad as not having a target at all. "You ever see a pitching coach tell a pitcher where not to throw it?" Dad asked us.

We shook our heads, although I, for one, had no idea what he was talking about.

"If a coach says, 'don't throw it low and outside,' what pitch do you think's going to come next?"

When we didn't answer right away, he shouted, "Low and outside! It's the last thing the pitcher thinks about, so of course that's what he's going to throw. The good pitching coach says, 'I want your best high heat, hard and inside,' and walks away. Well, that's the pitch he gets because it's the image the pitcher has in his mind.

"Whatever target your mind sees last is the one you're going to find, so you better make sure you're thinking about the right one."

All great players pick targets that are crazy small, just like Dad's "mound" one yard short and two yards left of the flag at Winged Foot. When Greg Norman was the top-ranked player in the world, he would pick targets so minuscule you had to strain to see them. At the eighteenth at Carnoustie, for example, most players use the large Rolex clock atop the clubhouse and hotel as their target from the tee. Greg chooses the top left pane in the window of a third-floor hotel room. He also earned a few chuckles from golf writers at the U.S. Open when he claimed to have hit a shot "a hundred thirty-three and a half yards." But to Greg, and players like him, there was nothing funny about that kind of precision. The best in the game pick small targets, focus exclusively on hitting those targets, and are not satisfied until they achieve perfection.

The greatest example of this that I witnessed firsthand came at the 2000 Open Championship at the Old Course in St. Andrews, Scotland. Tiger Woods, coming off a record-setting win at the U.S. Open, was striking the ball as well as anyone I'd ever seen. We had worked for several weeks on a particular shot for this tournament, one with a flatter trajectory that would bore through the gusting winds that whip off the Firth of Forth. Standing on the range prior to Thursday's opening round, I saw that Tiger had not only perfected the shot, he looked as though he'd been playing it his whole life. I noticed something else, too: I saw that Tiger no longer had to think about the swing; he was totally committed to his target. On Thursday, as he hit one driver after another, I realized that his target was the first zero on the three-hundred-yard sign. Every shot—low fades, high draws, and boring straight shots—flew over the center of the sign, bisecting the zero. Most players would have been happy to hit it somewhere near the sign, but then most players would have been happy finding only half a dozen bunkers at St. Andrews for the week. Tiger expected to hit every drive over that zero, and he played seventy-two holes on one of the most bunkered courses in the world without hitting one shot in the sand. He won by eight strokes.

And then there's Ben Hogan. In his only trip to the Open Championship, he chose to aim for the rough at the par-five sixth at Carnoustie, hitting his tee shot between the out-of-bounds stakes and the fairway bunkers, an area about fifteen yards wide. This shortened the hole considerably and gave Mr. Hogan the option of going for the green with his second shot. Most players wouldn't have considered hitting to an area that small. But Mr. Hogan wasn't trying to hit it in a fifteen-yard-wide area; he was trying to hit a spot less than a yard wide. The out-of-bounds stakes and the bunkers never entered his mind because they weren't on his target line.

Dad always told us, "Target-oriented players figure out how to get it in the hole, even when they're not swinging well. Swing-oriented players can't get it in the hole when they're hitting it perfect, and ball-oriented players have no chance."

I always thought Dad's line, "If you aim at nothing, you're always going to hit it," was great for golfers who were paralyzed by too many swing thoughts. I can't remember the number of times I've said things to students like, "If you're aiming at the condos you're hitting it great," when condominiums surrounded the driving range. But it wasn't until many years later that I discovered the life lessons hidden in Dad's prophetic saying. If you play a golf shot without a target in mind, the odds of ending up in a good place are remote. What I learned the hard way was that if you don't have a target for your life, you're also going to end up in some bad places.

As a young man my life "targets" were fast cars, good wine, a game to bet on, some cash in my pocket, and an afternoon tee time. Goals for next year, or the year after that, were the furthest thing from my mind. If something didn't satisfy me immediately, it wasn't on my radar. Dad saw this, and he did his best to steer me in the right direction. He would chew me out whenever I stayed out late and give me grief about not setting priorities for my life. "Did staying out make you smarter or richer?" he would ask after I'd pulled an all-nighter. He also used his biting tongue to remind me how good I had things while I was living at home. Many times I would be in the grillroom at Winged Foot and he would walk by and say, "Don't you wish you could afford to live the life you're living?" He meant to use the needle as a teaching tool. Life in the real world was harder than the life I had, a fact I would learn on my own soon enough.

We lived five miles from Winged Foot in the summer and fall, and I was at the club almost every day, playing, practicing, and enjoying the company of men and women I never would have met had it not been for my father. In the winters, Mom packed up the stationwagon, got our school transcripts, and closed up the New York house, and we traveled to Florida or California for Dad's winter jobs. Only one or two years did I start and finish a year in the same school. Most of the time, we started in New York and transferred to Florida, where we lived on the grounds of the Seminole Golf Club. We stayed there until the spring, and I finished the school year back in New York.

I traveled with Dad to the majors in the spring and summer, and I walked the fairways with him in most every event he played. Our family knew all the great golfers of the twentieth century because (with the exception of Bobby Jones and Walter Hagen) they had either come to our house, or played golf with Dad, or both. Mr. Hogan taught me the old Cow Town method of grilling steaks when he came over for a barbecue one night: "You cover it in salt," he said while my dad looked on in horror. "Then you put it directly on the coals." Mr. Hogan took the rack off the grill and laid his steak directly on the simmering charcoal. "Two minutes on each side . . ." he flipped the steak and timed it to the second, ". . . scrape off the salt, and she's done."

Most men of my generation would have killed for the kinds of experiences I had growing up. I responded to my upbringing by becoming a rebellious teen, pushing Dad's car down the driveway in the middle of the night to slip out on the town, making an ass of myself at every turn, and generally doing everything I could to exert some measure of misguided independence. I thought I was trying to carve out my own moniker as a man. In truth, I was an undirected, unfocused hellion, the kind of kid I probably would have choked if I had been my father.

After high school, I went to the University of Houston, one of the best golf schools in the nation, where I hoped to play on the team. Two weeks in, I played one bad round in a qualifying tournament at River Bend Country Club, broke every club in my bag, threw the heads into a pond, and went to California. Dad called the police, campus security, the highway patrol, and everyone else he could think of to find me. When I ran out of money, I didn't mind being found.

A year later, I enlisted in the army.

I could have gone into the special services sector and been a golf pro at one of the bases—that offer was on the table—but that wasn't what I wanted. Golf had ruled every aspect of my life to that point. It had dictated where I lived and where I went to school, what I did in the summer, and what I talked about with the family at the dinner table. Most important, the game had defined my relationship with my father. Our bonding had come on the lesson tee or in the fairways, places where he was a giant of unquestionable stature. By the time I was in my late teens, I wanted to get as far away from golf (and by extension, my father) as possible. I didn't know what my target was, but I knew what it wasn't. I didn't want to be known as Claude Harmon's son. And I wanted to do so far away from the lush fairways of Winged Foot. I signed up for the infantry and got married over my parents' objections.

For two and a half years my wife and I lived at Fort Richardson, Alaska, where the golf season lasted about three weeks, assuming you could find a course. From early October through the first of May, the days were short to nonexistent, and going outside could result in an ear falling off from frostbite if you weren't careful. In the summer, the sun never set, but I didn't spend a lot of time hitting golf balls at midnight. Infantry training was tough and time-consuming, so golf, even for recreational purposes, took a backseat.

I grew up fast in those first two and a half years, and even faster in the last six months of my tour. With half a year left to serve, I was shipped overseas to frontline infantry duty in South Vietnam.

Almost four decades later, I still don't talk about my combat service. Like many who were there, the memories are too personal and in some cases too hard. I lost friends and saw things that no man should ever see. I'm proud to have served my country, and I am honored to be a war veteran, but to paraphrase Dick Winters, I don't want my grandchildren asking me if I was a hero in the war. I wasn't. But I served in the company of heroes.

Three years in the military will do wonders for a young man's attitude and outlook on life. I was no exception. When I got out, I couldn't get back on the golf course fast enough. I realized what Dad had been talking about when he said, "Don't you wish you could afford to live the life you're living." The life I had lived in the final months of my military service was not something I would wish on anyone. My father's lessons about life, and the admonitions he had given me about my rebellious behavior, began to make sense and I realized that playing golf and being around golfers was a pretty good life after all.

Dad never kidded me when I was on active duty. In hindsight I'm sure he was worried sick about me every day I was overseas. But after I got out, he started joking about the clubs I'd broken in Houston. He embellished the story, saying they were the same irons he had used to finish third in the 1959 U.S. Open. They weren't, but it made the story better. Then he would say, "When Butch signed up, I told him I wished he'd joined the navy. Then maybe at least he could have gotten my clubs back."

I worked hard on my game after being discharged, and in the fall of 1968, I actually earned my tour card. But even in those days, after Arnold Palmer, Jack Nicklaus, and Gary Player brought professional golf into middle-class living rooms through television, the tour still wasn't what it is today. Guys who were not top-sixty money winners (guys like me) were known as "rabbits," hopping from Monday qualifier to Monday qualifier in the hope of making it into the field. If you played well on Monday, you got to play on Thursday and Friday in the first two rounds of the tournament. If you played well in the first thirty-six holes, you made the cut and got to play the weekend. Making the cut exempted you into the following week's event, which kept you out of the Monday qualifier. But if you skipped a week, you were back out on Monday trying to play your way in. We drove to every tournament, carpooling when we could and staying in the cheapest motels we could find. There were no seven-figure equipment deals, no car companies throwing keys our way; nobody traveled with an entourage. Jack and Arnold had their own airplanes, for sure, but most of the tour flew coach when they flew at all; rabbits rode the roads and prayed that their car tires held out. There were no swing coaches on the ranges every week, and in deference to my good friend Jackie Burke who said it first, we all had the same sports psychologist: his name was Jack Daniel's.

I struggled on tour for three years, winning one satellite event, the B.C. Open, and missing more cuts than I care to remember. It was a hard life, one I wouldn't want to repeat and one that definitely did not suit a man with a family. By that time I had two small children—a daughter, Michaele, and a son, Claude III—and few prospects for making a decent living as a tour player. So when the opportunity came up to take a teaching job in Morocco (a situation I will explain in greater detail a little later), I jumped at it. I lived in North Africa and worked as the private instructor for King Hassan II for five years, and I wintered there for five more years.

Then, in 1970, right before I went to Morocco, my mother passed away from cancer, which was a terrible blow, one I didn't get over for many years. Soon after she was gone, I returned home to the States and took a head professional job in Bettendorf, Iowa, at Crow Valley Country Club, one of the courses that for years hosted the Quad Cities Classic. Shortly thereafter, I made at least a triple bogey in my personal life. I started drinking more than normal and gambling away money I didn't have. I went through a less than easy divorce, and I ran my life into a ditch I had no way of getting out of. The only bright spot, and the only time I was happy during that period, was when I struck up a relationship with a college student from the University of Iowa—Christy Bohl—whom I would later marry. Much later.

The light Christy provided didn't last long enough. The club did not renew my contract, which was no great surprise, given how I had performed for them, and I found myself with no money, no job, no assets, and no way to repay the money I owed others. I hadn't conducted myself in a manner that the members of my club were entitled to, and I deserved to be fired. Losing Mom had been hard, but that was no excuse for the kinds of things I was doing. I behaved like the same directionless raging bull that had thrown Dad's clubs into the pond. The members at Crow Valley showed incredible restraint in tolerating me as long as they did. The Butch Harmon of today wouldn't have put up with the Butch Harmon of that era for more than a day or two.

At the time I didn't understand what was happening to me, but I knew I couldn't have been lower. Broke, alone, unemployed, homeless, and in debt, I had to make the toughest calls of my life—calls that should have been the easiest. When I couldn't pay my debts, I had to ask my father and brothers for help. Those calls were hard, not because I thought my family wouldn't help—I knew they would—but because I had to admit failure. I was the oldest brother, the one who was supposed to set the example. I also carried my father's name and had spent most of my life insisting that I knew better when it came to how to live. Now, I was worse than broke. I owed more money than I could make, and I had no means of supporting my children or myself.

My finger felt like it weighed a hundred pounds as I dialed my brothers' phones. When I told Dick what had happened, he said, "Get down here. You can live with me, and we'll work something out." He would have it no other way. Dick always looked out for the rest of us. He was more like Mom than the rest of us in that respect, and each of us saw our mother in him every time we got together. The fact that he opened his home to me and helped me get back on my feet is something I will never forget.

Craig was my second call. The first question out of his mouth was, "How much do you need?" I couldn't see through the phoneline, but I knew he had already taken out his checkbook. There is no finer friend to have than Craig Harmon, a fact that is reflected in his thirty-year tenure at Oak Hill Country Club. He is a giver, the kind of man our parents had wanted all of us to become.

The call to Dad had to be the toughest. I didn't realize it at the time, but I still wanted desperately to please him. The thought of going to him with hat in hand at that stage in my life—after having been a tour player and being the official instructor to His Majesty the King of Morocco—made me feel about as worthless and helpless as a man could feel. I knew that he had every right to say "I told you so," but he did nothing of the kind. Instead, he brought tears to my eyes by saying, "I'm proud of you for calling me. Now, let's get this thing worked out."

I moved in with Dick, and my brothers and father loaned me enough money to get out of debt. I also visited my dear friend Dave Marr, who was back in Houston at that time. Dave had retired from the tour as a player and become a golf commentator. With a dry Texas wit and a gift for knowing when to speak and when to let the pictures on the screen do the talking, Dave became one of the most recognized and honored golf broadcasters in history. He is still the benchmark for my work in the broadcast booth for Sky Sports. He was the closest thing I had to a big brother. Dave would baby-sit us when Mom and Dad went out and come over for dinner after work when Mom had cooked a meal. It was a way for him to get out of the apartment in the attic of the clubhouse, a way for him to feel part of a family even though he was many miles from his native Texas. As we grew older, Dave and I did all the things brothers would do: bicker, yell, laugh, and always love each other.

While we played countless rounds of golf together, there were only a couple of times when we were paired together on tour. One time that stands out in my mind came during the third round of the Atlanta Golf Classic at Atlanta Country Club. Throughout the day we had razzed each other on every hole, if not on every shot. Dave would miss a straightforward ten-footer and I would say "good putt"; I would hit it off the world and he would say "Oh, that's close." This went on all day. Then at seventeen, a short par-four with a slight dogleg to the left and a narrow, well-guarded green, I pushed my tee shot into the right rough, hit a huge slice with a seven-iron to get onto the green, and made a twenty-five-footer for birdie. Dave hit a perfect tee shot, a good iron shot to the center of the green, and three-putted for bogey. As we were walking off, he said, "That was the worst birdie I think I've ever seen." To which, I replied, "Really? What did you have?"

When the round was over we checked our cards in the scorer's trailer, and before we left, we hugged and kissed each other on the cheeks, a common practice in the Harmon household to this day. I told him I loved him, and he said, "You know I love you, brother."

The woman who had been our official walking scorer for the round couldn't believe what she was seeing. "That's amazing," she said. "I've been following you all day, and I thought you two hated each other."

"Ma'am," I said, "that man's like my brother."

"Well," she said, "you had me fooled."

What she didn't see, and what nobody realized, was the depths Dave would go to help my brothers and me, and what we would have done to help him if he had needed it. All the Harmons would have gone to the ends of the earth to help each other, and Dave was part of that family. He was also the only person I would listen to during my midlife misbehaving days. Dave would call me and, in typical big-brother fashion, say, "All right, I heard you've been screwing up again. What the hell's wrong with you?" And I would listen to what he had to say.

One day I listened a little more closely than Dave ever knew. It happened not long after I had moved to Houston to live with Dick and get my life back in order. I was looking for a job, and I asked Dave for an interview at his and Jay Riviere's golf-course construction company. In addition to working as a broadcaster, Dave built and managed golf courses in Texas. I hoped beyond hope that they would hire me.

Sitting in Jay and Dave's outer office—broke, tired, and as depressed as I'd ever been—I heard a conversation through the wall that will stick with me until the day I die. It was Jay, a good friend, but not someone who knew me as well as Dave did. Jay was a practical businessman, and he made a practical argument when he said, "David, we don't have a position for Butch."

"We'll hire him for golf-course construction," Dave said.

Jay answered, "But we don't have a golf-course construction job. We don't have anything open."

Dave said, "I don't care if we don't have anything. Create something. He's Claude's son. Remember everything Claude did for us? We've got to do the same for Butch."

That conversation will be seared in my brain forever. Dave could have patted me on the back, thanked me for coming, and sent me packing. Given my behavior at the time, I wouldn't have blamed him. But he was one of the people for whom the bonds of friendship and loyalty meant more than money. I know now that if Dave had been down to his last nickel he would have created a position for me.

I never let Dave know that I had heard his conversation with Jay. For a while it was too hurtful to think about how giving they were to me when I least deserved it. Then, I kept it to myself out of respect for Dave. He would never have wanted to talk about how he'd helped me, so I never told a soul what I'd heard him say until now. Dave passed away in October of 1997 at the age of sixty-three, after a long battle with stomach cancer. I felt that it was time to tell the story of what he did for me, so that a generation that never saw him play and never heard his buttery voice from the broadcast booth would know the kind of man Dave Marr was.

It was during the time I worked for Dave, as I was riding a tractor on the bare dry dirt of a newly shaped golf course, that I realized just how right my father had been in the lessons he had tried to teach us. In golf, and in life, if you aimed at nothing, there was no doubt you were going to hit it.

CLAUDE'S PEARLS

- If you don't have a target, nothing else matters. If you're aiming at nothing, in golf as in life, you're always going to hit it.

- Your body will react to what your mind sees. Make sure your mind focuses on the target you want to reach.

- The smaller the target, the more you have to focus to reach it. Make your target impossibly small and focus all your energy on reaching it.

- If you're practicing a golf swing, you're not practicing golf.

- Look at your target 90 percent of the time and at the ball as a last resort.

Six

"Why Get Mad?
You've Never Been Any Good"

Nobody wanted to win more than my father, and he taught all of his sons the value of being competitive. Every grade we made, every score we had on the golf course, every shot we hit in practice, every job we interviewed for, and every deal we entered was seen as an opportunity to compete.

"If you're not out to win, what's the point in playing?" Dad would say. This was his version of Vince Lombardi's "Winning isn't everything, it's the only thing" speech. Dad believed that every situation in life presented you with an opportunity to compete and to win. If you blew that opportunity, he was the first to let you know about it.

We competed for everything in our house. Who got to the breakfast table first, who told the most interesting story, who got the chores done quicker—these were all opportunities for the Harmon boys to compete. Dad spurred us on with both judicious praise and witty criticism. "How'd you let your brother clean his room faster than you? You're older. Doesn't that mean you should be faster and better at it than he is?" Or he would stand up in the living room and say "I want everyone to see what a great job Craig did on his homework today."

I got exposed to the thrill of victory early in life, during one of our winters at Seminole in Palm Beach, Florida. We lived in a split house—two dwellings under one roof, a common pre-WWII structure with the course superintendent's family occupying the other half of the house—just inside the gates of the club and adjacent to the sixth hole. As the members would play that sixth hole, they would send their caddies to find me. "Go get Little Butch and let's see him hit one," they would say. The caddies trotted off to find me (wasn't hard) and out I would run with my trusty seven-wood. The standard bet was a pack of Life Savers. If I could hit the green from a hundred yards out, I got the candy. Those Life Savers—things I could show off to my family as prizes I'd won with my golf skills—drove me to work on my swing. I loved winning, even when I was doing little more than entertaining some members. I started spending my days in the maintenance barn, waiting for groups to pass through. The caddies didn't have to call me anymore. When a group came to the sixth, I was there, seven-wood and ball in hand, ready to compete.

There was one problem: when I didn't win, I threw a fit and slammed the seven-wood into the dirt. Unfortunately, my temper did not improve with age. I guess I thought I should hit every shot perfectly, since I'd seen Mr. Hogan do it. When your model is the most precise ball-striker in history, your expectations are likely to be a little out of whack. When I couldn't reach the same level of performance or consistency I saw from Mr. Hogan, or my father, for that matter, my Vesuvian temper went on display for all to see. Dad had no tolerance for it, and he would become so angry that the veins on his neck would pop out as he ripped into me for my juvenile behavior. (I guess I came by my temper honestly.) But even though he chewed me out every time I threw a fit, I didn't get any better.

One year in a Metropolitan Golf Association junior event, I broke the shaft of my driver over my knee after hooking a ball out of bounds. Before I left the premises, the head pro had phoned my dad to tell him what a jerk I was. When I got home, Dad was sitting in the living room with his legs crossed and the newspaper in the lap. He played it cool, but I knew something was up. I could see the tension in his shoulders and neck. His back was straight and there was an uncomfortable stillness about the way he sat.

"How'd you do?" he asked.

The second he spoke, I could tell he already knew. The question was clipped. It came out as more of an accusation than a query.

"I didn't do any good," I said, trying to end the conversation as quickly as possible.

"Well, what'd you shoot?"

"I shot seventy-seven," I said.

"And?"

There was no use hiding it. He already knew what had happened. I confessed to breaking my driver.

Dad put the paper down, uncrossed his legs, and slowly hoisted himself up from his seat. I knew that another major-league reaming was coming. I deserved nothing less. But this time he just stared at me. It couldn't have lasted more than fifteen or twenty seconds, but it felt like a year. He was unnaturally still, and his hazel eyes were at once cold and sad.

"I don't know why you get so mad," he finally said. "You've

never been any good. I could understand Arnold Palmer's getting mad. He's good. But you're just Butch Harmon. What do you have to get mad about?"

That comment cut me to the quick. Arnold Palmer was my idol. I dressed like Arnold, hitched my pants like Arnold, and even tried to model my putting stance after him. To invoke Arnold's name was a sure way to poke the needle deep. Not only did I know that I was not in Arnold's league, I also knew that Mr. Palmer had never thrown a fit on the golf course in his life. The one time he had slammed a club into the ground, his father, Deacon, had marched onto the course, taken his clubs away, and told him that if he ever did anything like that again he would never play another round of golf. Dad didn't have to relay that story; he knew I already knew it. I went to bed fuming, which was what Dad wanted. If I got angry at the way I played, I should show it by working harder. Otherwise, I was nothing more than a punk kid throwing a temper tantrum.

I can't tell you how many times I've used Dad's line on hotshot young students who think they're God's gift to the game and who behave like two-year-olds when they miss a shot. It's one of my favorites. "Now, if you were Tiger Woods, I could understand your getting upset. He's good. But you've never done squat, so why the hell are you throwing a fit? You want to earn the right to have a temper tantrum? Go out there and work your butt off until you win something."

Of course, my father didn't reserve his sharp tongue for my temper tantrums on the golf course. I wasn't the best student in the world (a fact I tried to pawn off on changing schools every year), and Dad had no tolerance for my lackadaisical attitude toward the books. "Is there a bozone layer over your school?"

"A what?"

"A bozone layer," he said. "That's a fog of stupidity that keeps you from making intelligent choices. Unfortunately, it doesn't seem to be thinning anytime soon."

I didn't find his humor very funny, and I continued to behave like an idiot throughout my amateur and professional playing careers. At Briar Hall in Briarcliff, New York, at one of the state's biggest junior tournaments, I hit my approach on the fifteenth hole to within twelve feet for birdie. Dad was watching, so I felt pretty good. Then Dad walked away for a few minutes to check on my brothers. When he came back, I was twenty yards down the fairway with a wedge in my hands. He came running out onto the course. "What are you doing?" he said. "You know you can't practice during a round."

"I'm not practicing," I said. "I'm hitting my fifth shot."

"What are you talking about? You had a twelve-footer for birdie."

"Yeah, and when I missed it, I got mad and swatted the ball down here. Now, I'm just trying to finish."

He pointed that finger in my chest and said, "Well, when you do finish I'm locking your golf clubs in the trunk of my car."

The last serious fit I threw was when I broke all my clubs and threw the heads in the water when I was at the University of Houston. After that (and my stint in the military), my tantrums were limited to occasionally banging a club on the ground and saying words I wouldn't want my youngest son to hear.

But I wasn't the last Harmon my father had to worry about. My brother Billy's behavior on the golf course made me look like Mr. Manners. He started early, just like me. When he was six, Billy also had a cut-down seven-wood that he practiced with every day.

One afternoon he'd been hitting balls in the backyard, waiting for Dad to come home from work. When Dad pulled in, Billy charged the car and grabbed Dad by the shirttail. He wanted to show our father how well he had learned to hit it. On the first swing Billy cold-topped the ball and slammed the club into the ground.

Dad got down on his knees so he could meet Billy eye to eye. "It doesn't matter how good or how bad you hit it, that kind of behavior is unacceptable in our game," he said. "If you're going to be a golfer, you have to learn to behave like a gentleman, and gentlemen don't do what you just did."

The lesson didn't take for Billy, sadly. Several years later, when Billy was one of the best junior golfers in the country, he was playing in the Westchester Junior Championship at Westchester Hills. In the semifinal match, he was seven up after nine holes and had a six-footer for birdie to go eight up on the tenth. A group of members had started on the back nine, so when Billy and his opponent caught them, the foursome stood aside and let them through. Billy missed the six-footer, kicked his putter, swore, stormed off the green, slammed the putter against his golf bag, and walked to the eleventh tee without thanking or even acknowledging the members. Then he won the eleventh hole and closed out the match.

The finals were held that same afternoon. During that lunch break, Billy looked up and saw Dad walking into the clubhouse. Westchester Hills was a twenty-minute drive from Winged Foot. Billy thought Dad had come out to watch him play in the finals. By the time Dad got to his table, Billy knew from the body language that this was not a courtesy call.

"I want you to know that Jack Sabo (the pro at Westchester Hills) called me and told me what a jackass you made of yourself in front of the members this morning," he said. "So I took my lunch break to drive out here and tell you that I hope you lose every hole this afternoon." He turned to leave, and then turned back and added, "And if by some miracle you win this tournament, that trophy will never come into our house."

Billy won, and, sure enough, the trophy never darkened the door of the Harmon home.

Thankfully for my father, our brothers Craig and Dick weren't the hotheads Billy and I were. But they did have their moments. During the 1968 Metropolitan Amateur at Metropolis Golf Club, is Scarsdale, New York, Dick and Craig were playing each other in the semifinal match. Craig, who was seven down in the afternoon round, slowed the pace of play to a crawl in an attempt to disrupt Dick's rhythm. He took his time picking a club and walking to his ball. Dick would putt out and be teeing up on the next hole before Craig left the previous green. Finally, Craig hit his tee shot on the seventh into the eighth fairway, and he decided he had to go to the bathroom. He strolled off the tee long after Dick had reached his ball.

Dad, who had been keeping up with both semifinal matches from a golf cart, had seen enough. He met Craig in the rough, hopped from his cart, and with a couple hundred polite spectators watching, began pounding my brother on the shoulder with his fist. "What do you think you're doing?" Dad shouted. "You don't slow-play your brother! That's bush league! You want to win, play better! But you cut this crap out right now!"

Dick won the match six and five, but the story of the day was the unofficial slow-play warning Claude Harmon had given his son. On the way home, Craig almost caused a wreck when Billy started razzing him from the backseat about losing. Craig threw the car in park, reached around, and smacked Billy. "I have to take that crap from Dad, but I don't have to take it from you!" Craig yelled.

"You've got to want to win, but there's more to it than want," Dad would say. "If you've worked hard enough and smart enough, and you keep your wits about you, your competitiveness works in your favor. If you let your temper get away from you, you're as good as beat."

Dad took the game as seriously as anyone who ever played, but he always taught us to respect the game, respect our opponents, and respect ourselves while we were playing. I wished I'd heeded that lesson earlier in my career. Even Mr. Hogan tried to get me to calm down. During a round with my dad, Mr. Hogan said to me, "You've got a nice game, but you'll need to rein in that temper if you're going to go anywhere." I never did, and I never became much of a tour player because of it.

Part of Dad's intolerance for our antics had to do with preserving the integrity and character of the game. His hero growing up had been Bobby Jones, a man who had learned to control his own temperamental demons on the golf course. Jones was once banned from USGA events until he learned to control his temper (by none other than Herbert Walker, the USGA president the Walker Cup matches are named for and the great-grandfather of President George W. Bush). Jones got it together and went on to become the greatest amateur in history. Dad revered Jones as a young man and respected and admired him as an adult, especially after Mr. Jones helped my father into his Masters green coat.

Dad also respected how Jones maintained his dignity and discipline after leaving the game. In 1954, Dad hosted Mr. Jones at Winged Foot for the twenty-fifth anniversary of his 1929 U.S. Open win on the West Course. As part of the celebration, Tommy Armour, Craig Wood, and Gene Sarazen—three of the pros who played in that Open—attempted to make the twenty-five-foot putt on the eighteenth Jones had holed to win the title. After they all missed, Mr. Armour walked over to the cart behind the green where Dad and Mr. Jones were sitting. He handed Mr. Jones a replica of his old Calamity Jane putter and said, "You want to try it, Bob?"

By this time Mr. Jones was suffering the effects of syringomyelia, a rare congenital disorder that disconnects the motor nerves in the body from the brain. He could barely get out of the golf cart, much less make a putt. He didn't get angry at the request, and he didn't let his competitiveness get the best of him. Mr. Jones just smiled and said, "No, thanks. I've already made it."

That was the kind of class my father admired in men like Mr. Jones and the kind of behavior he expected from us. Once when Billy and Dad were playing together at Thunderbird, Dad hit a weak push with an iron, a bad shot that ended up in a bad place. He laughed at himself, put the club in his bag, and walked down the fairway. Billy said, "Dad, it doesn't bother you when you hit a shot like that?"

Dad said, "You know, son, some shots simply aren't worthy of comment. Everybody saw where it went. There's no reason for me to draw attention to the fact that it was bad."

They walked a few more paces, and Dad said, "You act the way you act when you hit it bad because you're trying to prove you're better than the shot you just hit. I don't need to make that point."

Billy didn't want to hear that, so he didn't respond. A few steps later Dad added, "The other reason is, if I hit a bad shot, I get it out of my mind and get into the solution mode as quickly as possible. You want to wallow in the problem mode as long as you can."

Dad had no patience for our impatience because he knew that our tantrums kept us mired in negativity. He wanted us to get out of the problem mode and into the solution mode the moment we hit the shot. "There's only one person holding the club, and only one person responsible for where the ball ends up," he said. "To get better, you have to take responsibility for the shots you hit and move on."

The quicker we could move on, the better. During my brief playing career, I called Dad whenever I was hitting it bad. Finally, he said, "You need to stop calling when you're hitting it bad and start talking to me when you're hitting it good. It's more important to remember what you're doing right than it is to worry about what you're doing wrong."

Dad's message was clear. Stop dwelling on the negative and start focusing on the positive. When you do, you'll find it easier to put bad shots behind you and move on to what's next. You can't take away the past. It doesn't matter if it's the golf shot you just hit or the bad life choice you just made. It's over. All you can control is what you do next.

And stop getting so mad. You're just trying to prove to the world that you're better than the last mistake you made. And some mistakes simply aren't worthy of comment.

CLAUDE'S PEARLS

- Competitiveness is great as long as it is kept under control.

- Showing your temper is like showing your rear end: everybody will look, but nobody really wants to see it.

- Some shots simply are not worthy of comment. Everybody can see where they went. There's no need to draw more attention to them.

- You want to win, just play better. Anything else you do to gain an advantage is bush league.

- Remember what you're doing when you're playing well, because you're going to need it when you start playing badly again.

———————

Seven

"Patience Is an Overrated Virtue"

During my days as a struggling touring pro, I talked to Dad about the troubles I was having and tried to pump him (and myself) up by finding a few positives. "I'm staying patient," I said.

"What did you shoot last week?" he asked.

I hemmed and hawed for a couple of seconds, knowing full well that Dad knew I'd shot a pair of seventy-fours and missed another cut. "I didn't play very well," I finally said.

"So that patience thing is working out for you, then."

"I didn't lose my cool."

"You didn't play worth a damn, either," he said. "I've always thought patience was an overrated virtue. You won't find many great ones who have much patience for anything. Now, they don't throw clubs and carry on when they miss a shot, but they don't sit still and wait for the game to come to them, either. The best always want to get better—not later, right now."

At the time I thought Dad was losing it. All I'd ever heard and experienced from working with great players was how patient you had to be in golf, how methodical your thinking had to be to score well, and how forcing things in golf would compound your mistakes. I still believe that to be true. You cannot force things in a golf tournament, especially a major championship. When you miss a fairway in the U.S. Open, you take your lumps, chip the ball back in play, make a bogey, and play the next hole. Trying to do too much can cost you the golf tournament.

But later I realized just how right Dad was and how I had been wrong all along. What I had always considered being "patient" in a golf tournament was not patience at all: it was simply being smart. Trying to hit a five-iron out of six-inch U.S. Open rough to an elevated green with a tucked pin is not an impatient play; it's a stupid one. Patience is accepting that certain things take time, like making a swing change (or, indeed, finding a medical break-through or developing new software). When I realized that I had been wrongly defining *patience*, I also realized that my father was right. The most successful people in any profession are the ones who refuse to sit still and wait for events to unfold around them. Their impatience forces them to make things happen—not later, but right now.

"Name me one great breakthrough that came from being patient," Dad would say. "You think Jonas Salk went home at five o'clock every day thinking, 'Well, I've just got to be patient'"?

He was right. Thomas Edison slept in his office for a month while perfecting the lightbulb. Mrs. Bell worried that her husband Alexander Graham might keel over dead from heart failure in the weeks leading up to the invention of the telephone. And Steve Jobs handed out T-shirts that said "100 Hours a Week and Loving It" to his engineers at Apple as they were creating the Macintosh.

Dad practiced what he preached. He was the least patient person I ever met. For example, after my mother passed away in 1970, Dad found himself having to raise my two younger sisters and manage the house for the first time in his life. He did a fine job until it came to shopping. Dad had never shopped, which was bad enough, but he also believed that you should buy ten of every item so that you would never run out. That's exactly what he and my sisters did the first time Dad went to the store. Among the three of them, they filled five shopping carts.

This wouldn't have been a problem had there not been a line at the checkout counter. Dad hated lines. Thirty seconds into any wait, he would start fidgeting, rolling his shoulders, and moving his head from side to side like a boxer between rounds. Oddly enough, he did not have this tic on the golf course. If play backed up and he had to wait on a tee, he would sit down, chat, stretch, and then stroll around taking practice swings until it was clear to play. Anywhere else, he was a nightmare. After about a minute in the checkout line, he turned to my sisters and said, "I can't do this. Let's go."

"But, Dad," my sister Claudia said, "what about the food?"

"We'll come back," he said.

They came back later and repeated the process, filling five carts and rolling them to the checkout line. Only this time Dad came prepared. After a minute in line, he took out his wallet, tapped the lady ahead of him on the shoulder, and said, "Excuse me, I'll give you five dollars if you'll let me cut ahead of you." He did the same to the next housewife, and the next until he had bought his way to the front of the line. He was happy, the ladies were happy, and the store manager was thrilled because Dad would have abandoned those carts again if he'd had to wait.

He was no better with my brothers. Dick, who has always been Mr. PGA of America through and through, tried to take Dad to several PGA seminars to help him keep his accreditation current. Dad had never held the PGA of America in high esteem, especially after they sent him a letter threatening to revoke his membership after he failed to fill out a boilerplate survey that asked questions like "Where is your facility located?" and "How many pull carts do you have?" Dad returned the threatening letter with a note that said, "If you don't know where Winged Foot is located, I suggest you contact the USGA. They have held a few events out here you might have heard of. As for pull carts, we don't have any. And enclosed is my membership card. If this is the kind of operation you're running, I'd rather not belong."

Dick clearly had a lot of work to do, so he started by taking Dad to the PGA Merchandise Show, an extravaganza held annually in January with every conceivable golf product and service on display in the million-square-foot Orlando Convention Center. Prior to Masters week, this was the only place where you could find everyone in the golf industry under one roof for three days. Even if you didn't buy anything, the Merchandise Show was a place where every golf pro could educate himself on the latest products and meet everyone in the business.

Dad had been there a total of twenty minutes when he said, "Okay, Dick, I'm ready to go."

"Ready to go?"

"Yeah, I've already picked up sixty yards. I've been to three booths and they've each promised me an extra twenty. I don't need any more. Let's go."

He had no patience for superfluous claims, especially from equipment manufacturers, and he refused to suffer fools. When a golf club salesman was showing the shop manager at Winged Foot a new fairway wood, Dad heard the fellow say, "You can't hook this club, guaranteed." Two seconds later Dad was in the salesman's face saying, "Guar—on—teeeeeed. Well, I'm going to want that guar-on-tee in writing, pal. I want your address and phone number, too, because when one of my students hooks this thing off the planet, I need to know where to find you." The salesman left without filling an order.

Dad also refused to coddle ignorance within his profession. He thought that if golf professionals were going to have the word *professional* attached to their names, they needed to know the game and business inside out. So when Dick took Dad to a rules seminar, and the first slide in the presentation showed red stakes, white stakes, and yellow stakes with captions that read "Red = Lateral Hazard, White = Out of Bounds, Yellow = Hazard," Dad stood up and said, "Let's go, Dick. Anybody who doesn't know what color an out-of-bounds stake is shouldn't be on the golf course, much less in the business. Let's go have lunch."

It was easy to see how my dad might bring a skewed perspective to the relative virtue of patience. But when I thought about his point, I realized that, despite his hangups and idiosyncrasies, I could not think of a single revolutionary breakthrough in science, technology, art, medicine, or sports that had come from a patient person. Maybe Dad was on to something.

I realized just how right he was when I started working with Greg Norman. Greg was (and probably still is) one of the least patient people I've ever met. He wants to get everywhere in a hurry—thus, the fast cars, fast boats, fast helicopters, and really fast jets—and he expects those around him to get things done in a timely manner, which means now.

I got to know Greg through another student of mine, Steve Elkington, the two-time NCAA medalist from the University of Houston. Steve had a great golf swing when he first came to me, and even though I had nothing to do with his natural ability and God-given sense of rhythm and timing, I felt good about the work we did together. Steve is an Australian, like Greg, so in the fall of 1991, after Greg had gone nineteen months without a win with a swing I thought had become too steep and handsy, and had dropped out of the top thirty on the money list, he approached Elk and said, "I'd like to work with one of the Harmons, Butch or Dick—which one do you think suits my game better?"

Steve said, "They're both great. You'd be happy with either one, but I think Butch fits your personality a little better. He won't BS you. You'll always get it straight from him." Dickie would have done the same. No BS was part of our makeup, but Steve was right about my personality being better suited for Greg. He was as impatient as I was, and he was a student who would challenge you, asking aggressive questions and expecting immediate, confident answers.

Greg didn't want an instructor who would be patient when analyzing his swing, because he wasn't going to be patient in making the changes. If he needed to incorporate a particular move into his swing, he would work like a madman, sometimes hitting a thousand balls a day until he had perfected it.

That same manic impatience carried over onto the golf course. He watched every leaderboard in every round because he wanted to know where he stood and what he needed to do to get to the top. Sports psychologists might have been counseling their clients not to watch the boards and to "stay in the moment," but not Greg. If he needed to make three or four birdies to take the lead, he wanted to know about it. More times than I can remember, he did whatever it took to climb to the top.

For years I had been impressed by Greg's ability to drive the golf ball long and straight, hitting it hard when he had to without losing control. He was, in my estimation, the greatest driver of the golf ball in history with a wooden driver. But I'd also watched him blow tournament after tournament with his irons, often losing the ball to the right. With all due respect to Jack Nicklaus, there is no way he should have won the 1986 Masters. Norman was playing great and only needed pars on the last two holes to win. But as happened time and time again, Greg drove it in the center of the final fairway and flared his approach shot well right of the green. He failed to get up and down, and Jack's miracle major was complete.

I had studied the swings of all the great players, and Greg was no exception. In addition to having spent many hours memorizing the swings of the greats from my dad's generation, I had watched Arnold Palmer, Jack Nicklaus, Gary Player, and Billy Casper in the sixties; Tom Weiskopf, Tom Watson, and Johnny Miller in the seventies; Seve Ballesteros, Tom Kite, Nick Faldo, and Nick Price in the eighties. I had memorized more swings than most people had ever seen. And I had always appreciated great players' abilities to hit the ball long and straight in pressure situations. When he finally came to me, I had seen enough footage of Greg Norman that I knew exactly what we had to do.

In our first session together, Greg hit a few shots while I watched. Then he said, "What do you see?"

I said, "I see somebody who needs to read his own book."

Greg was the author of *Shark Attack,* a book that emphasized the fundamentals.

"What are you talking about?" he said.

"You're not doing anything you said in your book," I said. "You're standing too far away from the ball at address; you're too steep on your takeaway; and you're trying to manipulate the club through impact with your hands. You need to go back to basics. Your fundamentals are bad."

This was a gamble, but one I was willing to take. Greg either wanted an instructor who was honest, straightforward, impatient, and who wouldn't pull any punches, or he didn't. I intended to find out which one in our first meeting. Dad's students loved his impatience and his bluntness, but Dad had a green jacket in his closet. When the same kind of pathological truth-telling came out of Butch Harmon's mouth, some viewed it as brash and off-putting.

It was hard to tell how Greg took it. He didn't say much. I'm sure other instructors had stroked him like a Persian cat, but I wasn't that way. His steep swing had worked as long as his hands squared the clubface. Under pressure, that didn't happen. The clubface stayed open, and the crucial shots squirted right. He needed to hear that without any frills.

I handed Greg a two-iron and said, "Stand tall, get closer to the ball, relax your hands, and swing as hard as you can."

Immediately, he hit a series of towering iron shots straight downrange. Then we worked on his grip and posture, on shortening his swing, leveling his shoulders, and flattening his plane. I wanted Greg to stop relying so much on his hands to swing the golf club. He had played great for a long time being a "hands" player, but that swing was beginning to fail him. If I could get him to use his lower body more and his hands less, I knew we could stop those iron shots from flaring to the right.

One of the phrases I heard my father use over and over in his teaching was, "If your fundamentals are sound, hitting the ball hard shouldn't cause you to lose control." That was what I told Greg, and it was what we worked on for the first year we were together.

He worked as hard as anyone I've ever seen. After he stood taller and crowded the ball, the first shot with the two-iron flew straight and so long that I think it surprised Greg. He hit another shot and another, all long and on line. We were on track, and I knew that Greg and I would be together for a while. That said, what I didn't realize was how demanding Greg would be. He is one of the most focused men I've ever been around, and because he demands perfection from himself, he also expects it from those around him. When he worked out, he went at it like a body builder, spending hours in the gym. He even put exercise equipment on his airplane so he wouldn't have to sit during flights. In business, too, he was as impatient as a three-year-old. He learned more about wine making in one year than most people could learn in a decade. He knows how many stitches per inch go into every one of his Greg Norman Collection shirts, and he can talk for hours about wicking polymers. That can be tough when you're working with him, but I was willing to go at it just as hard as he was. Once he believed in what we were doing, he committed himself fully to the changes and hit thousands of balls until he had perfected the swing.

He won nineteen times, including one major championship and one Players Championship, after we started working together. The breakout came in a tournament he did *not* win: the 1992 Open

Championship at Muirfield. Greg finished in the top twenty, but when he came off the course he said, "This is it. We're back. I just put on a clinic out there for seventy-two holes. Nobody will know it, but I did. We've turned the corner." These were not the words of a patient person. Two months later he won the Canadian Open, and six months after that he shot a course-record sixty-two in Miami to come from behind and win at Doral. He had shot a sixty-three in December of 1992 to catch Nick Faldo at the Johnnie Walker Classic, but lost in a playoff and had runner-up finishes in New Orleans and at the Western Open. He had, indeed, turned the corner. I believed him when he said that 1993 would be his year.

Unfortunately, he didn't play well at Augusta in 1993. I think the biggest disappointment in Greg's career has been his inability to win the Masters. He certainly had his chances. Everybody remembers Larry Mize's chip-in on the second playoff hole to beat him, but I always thought that Greg shouldn't have been in the playoff in the first place. He should have won the tournament in regulation, just as he should have won in 1986. The fact that he put himself in a position to lose put Larry in the position to hit that miracle shot.

In 1996, Greg's Masters collapse was painful to watch. He was thirteen under and leading Nick Faldo by six when he teed off on Sunday. On the first tee I could tell there might be trouble. He drove it left into the trees, hit his second shot short of the bunker, pitched on, and two-putted from seven feet for an opening bogey. He hit his second shot at the second into the gallery on the left. He hit another shot left on the par-three fourth and yanked his second shot on the par-five eighth into the trees. He pulled an iron into the tenth, making another bogey. He was fighting his swing and trying to hold on, neither of which worked very well. When he three-putted the eleventh for another bogey, Greg lost the lead for the first time all week. When he hit his tee shot in the water on the par-three twelfth, everybody knew the tournament was over. The Augusta patrons, always the most knowledgeable and courteous in golf, were virtually silent. It sounded more like a funeral than a golf tournament. As they walked off the eighteenth green, Faldo, who had just won his third Masters title, put his arm around Greg and said, "I don't know what to say. I just want to give you a hug." I think everyone in golf felt the same way.

Greg had another chance to win the Masters in 1999 when another of my students, José Maria Olazábal, beat him. Greg won't admit it, but after that I think he started believing he was cursed at Augusta. Once that thought crept into his head, it became a self-fulfilling prophecy. Despite eighty-eight worldwide wins and four years as the number-one player in the world, Greg never won the tournament he wanted most, and that probably bothers him to this day.

While not many people noticed, Greg was playing better than anybody in the world by the summer of 1993. The fire had returned, and I could tell that something special was on the horizon. What I couldn't have guessed was that it would come at the Open Championship at Royal St. George's, a golf course Greg didn't particularly like, and during a week when he didn't feel comfortable about his swing right away.

We arrived in Sandwich, a relatively small village about seventy miles south of London, early in the week to get in as many practice rounds as possible. The golf course—the southernmost links on the Open Championship rotation—would be called "quirky" if you were trying to be nice, and "goofy" if you were really honest. It definitely had more humps, bumps, and potential bad bounces than any other major championship venue. All links courses have mounds and valleys, but Royal St. George's looks like a three-hundred-acre seaside farm that has contracted the mumps.

Greg entered the week not striking the ball as well as he had throughout most of the season. He was having trouble keeping his body tall and moving through impact, a constant struggle for him even when he was scoring well. He also had a tendency to get his swing plane too upright. His hands sometimes looked like they were over his head on the backswing and followthrough. One of the first things I had him do when we started working together was stand taller at address and flatten his swing plane by swinging around his body. When he did this Greg's hands were more relaxed and less active through the hitting area, and he did not put an exorbitant amount of spin on the ball. One of the big criticisms of Greg's game early in his career was that he spun the ball too much. Many times he would fly his shots beyond the hole and spin the ball back off the front of the green. Flattening his plane allowed him to relax his hands, which allowed him to control how much he spun the ball.

On Wednesday of Open Championship week, he struggled a little with those changes, which was not unusual. Dad always said, "If you have a natural tendency, even if it's a bad one, you're going to have it your entire life. That's why I fought a hook twenty years after I hit my last one. If you have a natural problem, you're going to fight it your whole life. Just accept that fact and work with it." Greg wanted to swing the club high with his hands, and no matter how hard he worked to change it, he was always going to have periods of relapse.

A few minutes into our practice session I said, "We need to work on our ball-above-your-feet drill." It was something I had Greg do quite often. Having the ball above his feet forced him to stand taller and allowed him to release the club and keep his arms moving around his body. It was more of a followthrough drill than anything, but it always seemed to improve his impact position.

"Where are we going to do it?" he asked.

"There are mounds all over this place," I said. "We ought to be able to do it somewhere."

The only place we could find was a small mound to the right of the designated practice area. We moved so far right that we were on the other side of the equipment trailers that lined the right side of the range. Every equipment company brought a tractor trailer rig to the Open so players could get new shafts of a replacement club on the spot. They parked those rigs along the right edge of the "practice ground," which is what Europeans call the driving range. Greg moved beyond those equipment trailers and began hitting three-irons with the ball about twenty-four inches above his feet. For fifteen minutes he hit shot after shot over the equipment trailers and back onto the range, working with the same fury that marked our entire time together. This move produced the desired result. Greg regained the feel for standing tall, flattening his plane, and moving his body through impact.

Then a committeeman from the R&A showed up and tested Greg's patience. "Sorry, but you can't hit balls here," the committeeman said.

Greg barely looked up as he said, "I have to. This is the only place where I can get this kind of lie. I need this spot to get my work done."

The committeeman wasn't interested in Greg's getting his

work done, and a brief power struggle ensued. Finally Greg said, "What's wrong with my hitting from here, since you can't provide an adequate alternative to this lie?"

Semi-flummoxed, the committeeman said, "We can't control the crowd here."

Greg shook his head, raked another ball over, and said, "Butch and Tony [his caddy] will take care of the crowd. I'm getting my work done."

I looked back at the overflowing gallery and wondered exactly what Tony Navarro and I were going to do if they rushed us. Thankfully, I didn't have to find out. We worked in that area for over an hour without further incident.

Greg shot a sixty-six on Thursday and shared the opening-round lead, even after starting the tournament with an ugly double bogey on the first hole. From that point forward he played one of the greatest major championships I've ever seen, a tournament that included a final-round sixty-four in a thirty-knot wind and a missed fourteen-inch putt on the seventeenth for his only bogey of the day. That final day remains the finest round of competitive golf I've ever witnessed (and I've seen some awfully impressive ones). The fact that Nick Faldo teed off Sunday with a one-shot lead, shot sixty-seven, and lost says a lot about what Greg did that windy afternoon in southern England.

I was not alone in my assessment. Bernhard Langer, who was paired with Greg that Sunday, shook his hand on the eighteenth green and said, "That's the greatest golf I've ever seen. You deserve to win." And at the awards ceremony, ninety-one-year-old Gene Sarazen called it "the most awesome display of golf I've ever seen." Gary Player said, "It's the best golf I ever saw played at the Open."

Greg even impressed himself. Afterward he said, "I'm not a

man who tends to boast, but I was in awe of myself out there. I have never before gone around a golf course and not had a single mis-hit. Every drive and every iron were perfect. It was like playing a game of chess. I had a perfect angle to every flag."

A lot of players would have experienced a letdown after that kind of major victory, but winning sparked Greg to work harder. He won the Taiheiyo Masters in Japan later that same summer and ended the year by winning the PGA Grand Slam of Golf. In 1994 he set a still-unbroken tournament record to win The Players Championship. Then he won the Johnnie Walker Classic to become the number-one player in the world.

Throughout my time with Greg I would regularly catch myself uttering words and phrases that my father had used with me. "Your hands move much faster when you try to keep them passive" was one of Dad's favorites that I used time and time again. But the most important lesson Dad taught me that helped me with Greg was to be confident in my analysis, to never fear telling a student what I thought, and to remember that patience was an overrated virtue rarely found in the best of the best.

It's a shame that my relationship with Greg ended over something as silly and insignificant as a clothing contract, but I think the way we parted emphasized Greg's impatience. It happened in August 1996, during the week of the PGA Championship at Valhalla in Louisville, Kentucky. Because it was another major championship, Greg had answered approximately one million questions about his loss to Nick Faldo in the Masters that previous April. Even though he was the consummate professional when it came to dealing with the media, his nerves were raw. I can't say that I blame him. I couldn't have shown anything approaching the kind of methodical calmness Greg displayed when rehashing his Augusta collapse over and over.

I knew this and was sensitive to Greg's feelings. What I couldn't have anticipated was how he would react to conversations I had with a couple of clothing representatives. Nike had approached me with an offer. By that time, I had been teaching Tiger Woods for three years, and everyone knew that Tiger was going to turn pro in another three weeks. Nike was the leading candidate in the bidding war for Tiger. They wanted to sign me to a clothing contract prior to closing their deal with him. The offer was good, but not substantial by endorsement terms today. They would pay me some cash and provide me with a wardrobe.

I was flattered to get the offer, but I held the Nike rep off because Reebok was the licensee for the Greg Norman Collection at the time. They had provided me with clothing for years. I felt obligated to inform Reebok of the Nike offer and give them an opportunity to match it. I certainly wasn't contractually obligated to inform Reebok of any other discussion I was having, but I felt like it was only right to let the people who had been so good to me know what their chief competitor had offered. Reebok and their representatives had been very generous, and I felt a sense of loyalty to them.

I also didn't want to show up on the range one day wearing Nike clothing when Greg had given me so much signature clothing and provided me with so many opportunities. So I approached Richie Woodworth, head of the Greg Norman division of Reebok at the time, and said, "Richie, I have this offer from Nike. I'm not comfortable taking my discussions with them any further without telling you, because you've been so good to me." Then I shared the deal terms with him and said, "Would you have any interest in matching that deal?"

He said, "We can't give you cash, but we can book you for a couple of outings that will end up giving you that same amount. Will that work for you?"

"Absolutely," I said, and I walked away feeling as though I had done the right thing. I got to keep my relationship with Reebok without leaving a lot of money on the table. It made business sense and made me feel good about the loyalties I had protected.

Frank Williams, who was Greg's manager at the time, didn't see it that way. He literally sprinted to Greg's side and spun an incredible yarn. Frank told Greg that I had gone to Reebok behind Greg's back. He said I was trying to get Reebok to pay me for wearing Greg Norman clothing when it was Greg who had given me the clothes in the first place. Couched that way (inaccurately), I couldn't blame Greg for being livid.

Greg could have patiently waited to hear my side of the story, but that would have been out of character for him. You cannot expect someone who is demanding and driven in everything he does to suddenly become docile and indecisive. Greg was going to vent his anger over this, and he was going to do it right then. When I came out of a meeting at the Sky Sports compound, I found Greg on the sixth fairway at Valhalla, as far away from the clubhouse as you could get. When he saw me, he marched over double-time and yelled at me in a way I had never seen before. The primary gist of his rant was "Who do you think you are? Going to Reebok about paying you to wear clothes! I've given you those clothes! Who do you think you are?" He was so mad he was shaking.

I tried to explain, but I couldn't get a word in. He was venting, not just the frustrations from what he perceived as a slight from me but the four months of frustrations he had endured since losing the Masters. Finally I said, "Greg, this is Tuesday of a major-championship week. You need to have your mind on golf. I think I need to leave."

It must have continued to gnaw at him because he called my hotel room that night and chewed me out again, not giving me any opportunity to explain what had happened. After about five minutes, I simply hung up on him. And that ended my relationship with Greg Norman.

That fall, at the Tour Championship at Southern Hills in Tulsa, Oklahoma, I ran into Frank Williams and confronted him about what had happened. When I asked him why he would distort what had happened in Louisville, he got overly defensive and loud (the mark of a guilty man in my book). Later he told Greg that I had called him a name that one man might call another in Europe, but a word I wouldn't have used in a million years. What I had actually called him was a f-ing a-hole, words that passed my lips as effortlessly as water running downhill.

Two months later, Tiger and I went to Australia, and Greg confronted me yet again, this time accusing me of calling his manager that dirty European word. I didn't let him get away with it this time. I told Greg exactly what I'd called Frank, and why. "And if you don't believe me, ask your caddy. Tony heard every word of it," I said.

I figured that would be the last conversation I'd ever have with Greg. But a couple of years later at the Open Championship, he approached me on the range and said, "I owe you an apology. I had bad information, and I didn't give you the benefit of the doubt." He had since fired Frank Williams and learned the truth. "You had every right to approach Richie Woodworth, and I was wrong for what I said. I apologize."

I appreciated the apology, but what he said next meant more to me than anything. Just before he walked away, he shook my hand, and said, "I just want you to know, I've really missed your friendship."

We've been good friends ever since. Greg was under a tremendous amount of pressure during that time, and he let his frustrations boil over in a way that was completely out of character for him as a person. He was impatient, yes, but never impertinent. The man who looked me in the eye, shook my hand, and apologized was the Greg Norman I always knew. He was and is one of the classiest people in golf.

Once a summer my brothers and I host an event called the Harmon Cup, a small, private, invitation-only gathering for a dozen of our friends. The field includes people like Jay Haas and Craig Stadler, but also friends whose names you wouldn't recognize. The year after Greg and I finally shook hands and buried our differences, my brother Craig hosted the Harmon Cup at Oak Hill. Greg, as he had been several times, was on the invitation list. The pairings are usually a blind draw, but Craig almost fell over from a heart attack when I requested that I play Greg in the singles match.

"Do you think this is a good idea?" Craig asked Billy. "What do you think will happen?"

"I think they'll have a pretty decent match," Billy said. "Course if it comes to blows, I'll have to take the Shark. He's got a good eight inches on Butch."

"Oh, God," Craig said.

Billy could barely contain his laughter when he told me the story.

"Tell him to relax," I said to Billy. "If it gets that far, I'll take a three-wood to his knees."

Greg and I talked and laughed and enjoyed each other's company, just as we had when we worked together. I played well, too, which was an added benefit. Through thirteen holes I was five under par and one up on Greg. That's when I noticed that the conversation had quieted down. Mr. No Patience for Losing had his game face on. It wasn't until I pushed a ball out of bounds on the fourteenth and made double bogey that Greg started talking and joking again.

"Why, you S.O.B.," I said, "I get up on you, and you quit talking to me?"

"Hey, this is a match," he said, laughing. "Do you make every putt you look at?"

"I hope so," I answered. "There's only one hole on the green, and we're both aiming for it."

Greg won the match, and we had a great time.

I felt fortunate to work with a player of Greg's talents. I was also pleased with the run we had together, and I'm proud of the friendship we have today.

When it came to patience, I began to notice a pattern among the tour players whom I worked with and observed. Those golfers who insist on being patient and letting the game come to them rarely play up to their potential. They play well, maybe win a time or two, but they never reach the great heights their talents dictate. The Players who want to learn, get better, and win right now—this second, no waiting—are the ones who exceed their natural abilities and become the game's great overachievers.

Justin Leonard, for example, has all the patience of a kid with his hand over the cookie jar. When we first started working together, Justin knew he needed to change his golf swing to improve his distance and ball flight. This was not a decision that should have come easily. Justin had won a U.S. Amateur, an Open Championship, and a Player's Championship with a low ball flight, relatively short driving distance, an unbelievable short game, and the heart of a lion. By all rights, Justin Leonard should not have won as much had he had. He was a classic overachiever, a bulldog who worked as if each day were going to be his last. Justin knew that to take his game to another level—the level of multiple major champion and top-ten player in the world—he needed to hit the ball higher and fly it farther. Once that decision was made, he wanted it done right then: no waiting, no subtle baby steps. It took a year, a short time to make a major swing change, but Justin adapted. Now, he's playing some of the best golf of his life.

But the king of "Patience is an overrated virtue" has to be Tiger Woods, who would be hard pressed to call it a virtue at all. I used to love it when Tiger told the media that he was "really patient out there," right before telling me, "I didn't hit a single solid shot, and we're not leaving the range until we get it right."

When Tiger wants to do something with his golf swing, he wants it done now. No phasing it in and no long-term planning. Once he decides to make a change, he makes it fully and immediately. Then he works himself ragged until he perfects it, exhibiting little or no patience along the way.

When he first turned pro, Tiger had an average short game by tour-player standards and had a poor bunker game for a top-level player. Through sheer determination and an unquenchable quest for new information, Tiger built the best short game in the world, which he displayed in the 2005 Masters when he chipped in at sixteen from a dead-and-buried spot behind the green. That shot did not come about by accident, and he did not perfect it by being patient. Tiger refused to rest until he had reached his goals, one of which was to become the best short-game player in the world.

I never sought out Tiger Woods as a student. His father, Earl, came to me not long after Greg won the 1993 British Open. By then Tiger was a seventeen-year-old high school senior and the most decorated junior golfer in history. He had just won his third straight U.S. Junior title, becoming the first kid ever to three-peat in that event. He had been a first-team Rolex Junior All-American for four straight years—also a first—and *Golf Digest*'s junior player of the year for three straight years, becoming the first player to win three of those awards as well. A month after I got home from Southport, England, Earl called me after Tiger had lost his second-round match in the U.S. Amateur, which was being played at Champion's Club in Houston. Greg had gone out of his way to recognize me in the press after winning that Open Championship, which was very kind of him. Earl Woods had seen those comments and had been impressed by the changes I'd made in Greg's swing. He thought it was time for Tiger to advance to what Earl called a "pro's pro."

I invited both of them out to Lochinvar in Houston, where I was working at the time. We had lunch and, afterwards, I took Tiger out to the range and watched him hit a few shots. I had heard and read a lot about him, but I hadn't seen him swing. I never got out to junior golf tournaments—my brother Dick was the junior-golf guru of the family—and at that point Tiger hadn't played in any of the professional events I attended. When I saw him for the first time, there was no question I was watching something special. Tiger came out and hit balls in his tennis shoes, and it was like seeing a teenage Mozart at the piano or a young da Vinci with a sketchpad. At one point during that first session I said, "Tiger, Greg Norman has great hands, but you might have the best hands I've ever seen in golf."

He perked up. I could tell that that comparison got his attention. He wanted to hear more.

"I bet you can feel where the clubface is right before impact," I said.

"I can," he said, nodding.

"Can you make corrections with your hands before impact?"

"Sure," he said, shrugging, as if manipulating a clubhead moving at a hundred and thirty miles an hour so that the face was square at impact was no more difficult than eating a Big Mac.

"You'll need to work on that for the future. Your plane dictates the amount of hand action you need through impact. To be consistent you want your swing plane to square the clubface, not your hands."

Then we talked about the shots he liked to hit and the shots he never wanted to hit but occasionally did. I asked him to hit different shots—low cuts with a driver, punch-draws with a two-iron, a one-hundred-yard shot with a nine-iron. (I did film Tiger, a film I've kept all these years and one Tiger hates to see now because he was so skinny back then.)

I liked what I saw, and more important, I liked what I heard. Everyone knew the kid had talent, but I was amazed by his focus, his intelligence, his maturity, and his eagerness to learn. He was a sponge. Everything I asked him to do, he did. He asked all the right questions and absorbed every answer. He had an encyclopedic knowledge of the game and an intense and impatient desire to learn more. I asked him if he wanted to come back the next day. He did, and the second day we worked on his control. Tiger was always long, even as a skinny kid, but he had a tendency to lose shots to the right. His swing was so fast that his lower body often outpaced his arms and hands, and the club got "stuck" behind him, which meant he had trouble getting the clubface square at impact.

I felt good about the work we did, and I really enjoyed Tiger's and Earl's company. Earl didn't interfere in the lesson, and Tiger showed a tremendous amount of respect for both his father and me. It was evident from our first meeting that Tiger was not just a great golfer but also a great person. He listened, asked intelligent questions, said "yes, sir" and "no, sir," and was in every way appropriate. I had taught a lot of kids who had less talent than Tiger but who had more pronounced egos. It was refreshing to see someone as talented as Tiger who was also apparently grounded. Earl was also a solid man, someone who cared about his son, but who showed none of the signs of being a stage dad. I was impressed by both of them.

A week later, the phone rang. It was Earl. He told me he thought he had taken Tiger as far as he could, and he wanted to know if I would consider coming on board as Tiger's teacher. "I want you to take him to the next level," he said.

"It would be an honor," I said, but I still had some reservations. I recognized Tiger's talent, but the X factor was Earl. No one had to tell me how complicated father-son relationships could be, especially in golf families. My dad had been my primary instructor, and like all kids, I'd gone through a period during which I thought he was the dumbest rube who ever walked upright. Then there were times when I would have done anything in the world to please him. I pushed myself to show Dad what I could do, and I let my temper run away from me when I thought I wasn't performing up to his expectations. I knew all of these things because I had lived them, but I also knew that every son has conflicts with his dad. What I didn't know was how Tiger and Earl dealt with those conflicts. If Earl was overbearing, or if I had misread him in our first meeting and he was living vicariously through his kid, I didn't want any part of it. But if, as I suspected from our first meeting, Earl was doing the right thing, and if Tiger was playing golf for the right reasons and not just to please Earl, then I would love nothing more than to help.

I said to Earl, "I'm only concerned about a couple of things."

"What are they?"

"I know you've worked with Tiger all his life. He doesn't need to get mixed signals from you and me. You're his father. If you have a problem letting go, I understand."

"Nope, I'm turning him over to you," he said. "I won't undermine your authority when it comes to golf. You don't undermine mine when it comes to being a father."

"Deal."

"What's the second condition?"

"I won't charge you until Tiger turns pro. Then I'll send you a bill."

"Hard to argue with that," Earl said.

We got along great from that moment forward.

My first impression proved to be correct. Earl was a good

man doing great things for his son, a family dynamic I could relate to. Earl sacrificed a lot for Tiger, and he did so with no thought of being rewarded at some point in the future. He did it because that was what he thought a father should do. I had lived with a man who made similar sacrifices, so I had great respect for Earl from the beginning. Earl and I also hit it off because of our shared experiences. We're both Vietnam veterans, both no-nonsense guys who had strong no-nonsense fathers who shaped our worldviews. We both believed that hard work and tenacity could overcome a lot of obstacles, and we both wanted to do what was right and best for Tiger.

I told Earl that it would be a three-year process, that Tiger should expect to remain an amateur until he was twenty, win as much as he could at that level, and then we would reevaluate. Everybody signed off on that plan, and we went to work. In the next three years, we worked primarily through phone and videotape. The times we did get together—at the majors, and a few other times throughout the year—he would absorb information like no one I'd ever seen.

Teaching smart, talented, and motivated players is the cherry on the sundae for any golf instructor. Too often, our days are filled by helping less than stellar athletes make modest changes to their games. When I was young, I would see my father teaching elderly women who had very little skill and even less potential. He would help them with their grips and setups and do what he could to help them make contact. One day I said, "Dad, why do you teach people who have no chance? Don't you feel like you're wasting your time?"

He lowered his voice, dropped his chin, and raised his brow as he cut a gaze straight through me. "If people want to learn and are willing to work, then I'm ready to teach them, no matter how good or bad they are. Everybody has had trouble with the game at some point. I get just as much joy out of helping a high handicapper get rid of the shanks as I do helping a tour player. My only criterion is their willingness to work on what I tell them. If they'll work, I'll teach. It's that simple."

It was that simple for me, too. As long as players believed in the things we were doing together and were willing to work hard to incorporate those things into their games, I was willing to do whatever it took. Tiger Woods was one of those self-motivated people who work at a manic pace. He was like Mr. Hogan in that respect. Dad used to tell me that players dreaded having hotel rooms near Mr. Hogan because he would be in the hallway putting all hours of the night. Walls were thin in those days, and it was not unusual for players up and down the hallways to hear the distinct sound of a putter hitting a ball at one in the morning. Mr. Hogan didn't care what time it was. If he needed to work on his stroke, he did it whenever and wherever he could. The same was true with Tiger. There were many times when I would be talking on the phone with Earl after dark, and I would hear the click of a club striking a ball. "What's that?" I'd asked.

"Tiger's hitting chip shots."

"In the house?"

"What are you going to do?" he'd say.

I didn't have to worry about Tiger working hard, and that hard work paid off in ways I could never have imagined. During our first three years together he became the first man in history to win three consecutive U.S. Amateur titles. Bobby Jones, who was never a professional and played in fourteen U.S. Amateurs, never did it. Jack Nicklaus only won two in a row. Arnold Palmer only won one. Tiger won the Amateur at every kind of golf course in the country—the Pete Dye–designed Tournament Players Club at Sawgrass in Ponte Vedra, Florida, the home course of the PGA Tour; the classic Donald Ross design of Newport Country Club in Rhode Island, where my brother Billy was the pro; and the tree-lined northwestern Witch Hollow course at Pumpkin Ridge in Oregon—and against every kind of opponent, whether young, old, slow, fast, short hitter, or long hitter.

During that time, Tiger and I worked on improving his control, especially with his driver, which was long but could go anywhere. His swing speed was so fast that he often had trouble getting the club to square up at impact. He also tended to let his head dip when he hit it hard. None of these problems was terrible. If you look at swing sequences of Tiger when he was a teenager, he had a good move. But to become the best in the world, and perhaps the best in history, we had to continually work.

Tiger won twice in his first seven starts as a pro. Then, in the first event of 1997, the Mercedes Championships at La Costa in Carlsbad, California, Tiger tied Tom Lehman, the 1996 Player of the Year, through three rounds when tour officials had to call the event due to rain. They found one dry hole, the 186-yard par-three seventh, for a playoff. With every golf fan in America watching, Lehman hit first and pulled his ball into the water. Tiger hit second and pulled his six-iron to within eight inches of the hole for birdie and the win. Networks that weren't carrying the event broke away from their NFL coverage to relay the news of Tiger's miraculous shot. In fact, Tiger hadn't made a great swing in the playoff, but rather had his best miss of the week. What he had meant to do was play to the right side of the green after Lehman hit it in the water. Instead, Tiger pulled the shot. Fans, therefore, saw him stuff a six-iron tee-shot inside a foot and knock out the reigning Player of the Year. The shot led the *SportsCenter* telecasts throughout the weekend.

By the time we got to Augusta for the Masters the first week of April 1997, Tiger was the hottest thing in sports and one of the biggest newsmakers of the year.

I was not surprised when Tiger won the Masters in his first professional try. For starters, he thought he was going to win, which was half the battle. Tiger has always been someone who responded when people said he couldn't do something: improving his short game, for example. A lot of people said he couldn't win the U.S. Open; that his irons were too erratic, and he missed too many fairways. When he won his first Open at Pebble Beach by a record-setting fifteen shots, he sent me a pin flag and a photo of him holding the U.S. Open trophy with a note that said, "Butchie, they said I couldn't win one of these." Some people said Tiger couldn't win the Masters in his first outing, too, because he was too young, too inexperienced, and not a good enough putter. He won by twelve and did not three-putt a single green in seventy-two holes.

The week after Tiger's Masters win, when he was on the cover of everything from *Money* magazine to *Redbook*, Tim Meadows and Tracy Morgan did a *Saturday Night Live* skit that became an instant classic. In the skit, Tiger, portrayed by Tim Meadows, says he wished his father hadn't Super-Glued a club to his hands, while Earl, as played by Morgan, calls Tiger "Gandhi . . . and whatnot." It was hilarious, and something that added some much-needed levity to what I knew could be a difficult situation in the future.

Tiger won the Masters with the swing we had built since he was seventeen. But we both knew that if he was going to continue winning—winning tournaments like the U.S. Open, where the fairways were narrow and the rough was thick—we needed to re-tool his swing, to shorten it, tighten it, and put the club on a slightly different plane so he could control his distances and shape shots when needed. Not a lot of people noticed this, espe-cially after Tiger demolished most of the records at Augusta Na-tional, but he and I knew that we still had work to do.

For the eight months between late August of 1996 when he turned pro and his record-setting win at the Masters in April of 1997, Tiger swung the golf club with almost perfect timing. His clubhead speed was faster than any tour player. The ball speed off the club approached two hundred miles per hour, so he had to have perfect timing to square the clubface at impact or the ball would go so far off line it might not come down on the golf course. I knew that this sort of timing was not always going to exist, and that Tiger's violent action through impact with his cur-rent plane would eventually cost him. Going after a drive with a swing speed of a hundred thirty-five miles per hour and a shut clubface produced some incredible tee shots. Hitting a five-iron, seven-iron, or nine-iron with that same swing produced the kind of inconsistent distances that would not work in the long term. If Tiger wanted to win multiple U.S. Opens and PGA Champi-onships, if he wanted to threaten Jack Nicklaus's record of eigh-teen professional majors and become only the fourth player in history to win all four professional majors in his career, we had to rebuild his swing for consistency.

A few weeks after the 1997 Masters I showed Tiger a film of his swing at Augusta. We went back and forth, watching his mo-tion in full speed, slow motion, and spot action, frame by frame. About twenty minutes into the session, his eyes got wide, and he said, "Butchie, we've got to change that position, especially at the top."

Three quarters of the way though his backswing, the shaft of the club was behind his right shoulder and the clubface was closed. This forced him to lift the club with his hands to finish his backswing. When he reached the top, the clubface was pointing straight up at the sky, a closed position. Because of the steepness of his swing plane and his almost unnatural ability to turn his shoulders well past ninety degrees on the takeaway, the shaft of the club was also pointed to a spot well right of the target at the top. Instructors refer to this position as "across the line," which means the club "crosses" the imaginary vector between the ball and the intended target. From this position, Tiger had to reroute the club to get it back on track on the downswing. Plus, having his clubface closed at the top and descending at such a steep angle caused him to hit his irons incredibly long because he was de-lofting them, turning a nine-iron into a seven-iron, and on up through his bag. This created havoc with his distance control.

A lot was made during the Masters about Tiger's hitting short irons into the par-fives. Famed sports writer Dan Jenkins wrote an essay in *Golf Digest* about how Tiger "overpowered" Augusta National. Jenkins compared the clubs Tiger hit into various holes with those Ben Hogan hit in 1953. Of course, Mr. Hogan hit balls that were 20 to 30 percent shorter than the ones played today, but that didn't matter. Fans saw Tiger hit a nine-iron into the par-five fifteenth for his second shot, the same hole where Jack Nicklaus nutted a three-iron approach on his way to winning in 1986 and where Mr. Hogan laid up more often than he went for the green in two. Tiger made it look like a short-iron par-four. He did this by hitting his tee shots down the right side and taking advantage of the spectator mounds. Tiger flew the ball so far off the tee that he could hit the downside of those mounds and use them as slingshots. Then he de-lofted his nine-iron and hit it upwards of 170 yards. This created the myth that Tiger was able to overpower Augusta National. He and I both knew that he was playing better than he knew how with a swing that would eventually falter.

Without any prompting Tiger saw the film of his tournament and said, "I won with perfect timing," he said. "If I don't have that, I've got no chance."

Tiger was one of the brightest students I'd ever taught. I was proud that he had seen the problem on his own. "You're right," I said, even though I knew how controversial the changes would be. Given what had just happened at the Masters, the very notion of changing Tiger's swing was considered radical by some, insane by others. Tiger was the hottest golfer in the world and maybe the most recognized and popular golfer in history. His incredible story, his ethnicity, his meteoric rise, and his charisma had everybody paying attention. A quick look at the media outlets he chose to visit after his Masters win tells the story. The all-news and all-sports channels wanted interviews. So did the anchors of the network newscasts and the late-night talk show hosts. Tiger and Earl chose to make their first post-Masters appearance on *The Oprah Winfrey Show,* a program with a predominately female, nongolfing audience. The Woods knew that Tiger transcended golf, and they wanted to let the nongolfing world get to know him.

That philosophy worked great until we started talking about the swing changes. Half his fans were novices. Explaining swing plane and clubface position to them was like trying to teach me to perform transplant surgery. The fans saw a kid who had won his first major by twelve shots. And they saw an idiotic teacher who thought we needed to change his swing.

One clever columnist likened the decision to change Tiger's

swing to Michael Jordan's deciding to shoot his jump shot left-handed, just for fun. It wasn't quite that radical, but I understood the criticism. Tiger had just demolished the world's best players in the world's most prestigious golf tournament, the one every great player wants to win. Weeks later, we were going through a major overhaul of his swing. I was being called the "Tiger killer," and the "man who painted a mustache on the *Mona Lisa*," even though it was Tiger who told me we needed to make the changes, not the other way around.

I knew the changes were necessary, but I thought we should make slow, incremental changes—improvements that would take years and wouldn't cause a major disruption in Tiger's game. What I didn't count on was Tiger's Greg Norman–like lack of patience. He didn't want to wait for a second to do what needed to be done.

"I know you want to do it piecemeal, but if we're going to make changes, let's make them. All at once. Now," he said.

I loved his enthusiasm, but I wanted to make sure he understood the consequences of what we were about to do. "It's going to be hard, and it's going to be controversial," I said. "In addition to the work you're going to have to do on the range, you're going to have to answer questions about what the heck we're doing. Every event you play in, you're going to be asked the same questions. 'What are you thinking?' 'Why would you change a swing that won the Masters?' 'Is it worth it?' You're going to get sick of hearing it."

"Let's do it," he said. "I'm ready."

First, we had to make sure Tiger's upper arms didn't stray too far from his torso at any point during the swing. He was especially prone to letting his right elbow get away from his body. That allowed him to get great extension on the backswing, but it also left him in a vulnerable position at the top. Once the elbows stray from the body, they tend to stay separated. Jack Nicklaus is the only noteworthy example of a great player who let his right elbow wander on the takeaway and returned it to the correct position on the downswing consistently. Every other great player in history has kept his right elbow reasonably close to his right side throughout the swing. This puts the club on the correct plane on the backswing and allows the clubface to rotate open on the takeaway and back to square on the downswing without any unnecessary manipulation of the hands. When Tiger let the right elbow get too far away from his body, the club strayed behind his shoulder and across the line.

We had to make sure Tiger kept his hands and arms in front of his torso throughout the swing. He generated so much speed by firing his lower body on the downswing that if the arms strayed too far behind him, they would never catch up on the downswing and he would spray shots to the right or be forced to manipulate the club with his hands. He had done the latter quite effectively at Augusta and on several other occasions in his rookie season.

The other thing I wanted to see him do was shorten his takeaway. A common misconception is that a good takeaway gets the club to parallel to the ground at the top of the backswing. In truth, many great players have never gotten the club to parallel, and only a few have ever gone beyond parallel. John Daly is an example of someone who takes the club back entirely too far, but John is talented enough to play with that motion. Most golfers would never make contact if they emulated John's takeaway, and a majority would hurt themselves. Tiger didn't need to take the club to parallel to hit the ball a long way. In fact, when he got it to parallel he tended to throw the club at the ball with his hands and spray shots off line. He had a great shoulder turn, and he unwound his lower body on the downswing faster than anyone in the history of the game. Shortening the swing so that the club never made it to parallel did not cost him any length, but it did wonders for his control.

It also improved the position of the club at the top relative to the target line. For every degree the shaft stopped short of parallel, it should also point a corresponding degree left of the target. So, if Tiger's backswing stops ten degrees short of parallel, the vector extending from the shaft of the club should point ten degrees left of the target. All of these things put the club in a position for maximum speed and consistency at impact; and while they sound incredibly complicated, Tiger knew exactly what he needed to do to get there, and he worked like a maniac to implement the changes.

The process took eighteen months. We worked with video in my teaching center and with drills during tournament weeks. I spend thousands of hours on the ranges at tournament sites, holding clubs at various angles to give Tiger visual cues about where the club should be at different points in the swing. It was tough and tedious, and he certainly wasn't patient during that time. I saw him throw clubs and vent his frustrations on the practice tee more times than I can recall. One time when he was alone practicing at his home in Orlando he got so frustrated that he threw his club down the range, got in a golf cart, drove out on the range, and ran over the offending club until the shaft broke. He also swore and kicked his golf bag. But he would always step up to the next shot more determined than ever to do whatever it took to get his swing right.

During that period he won only once, at the BellSouth Classic in Atlanta, and he lost his world number-one ranking to David Duval. Any other player might have doubted himself—and me. But at the beginning of 1999, Tiger began to feel comfortable with what we had done. That year he won eight times, including his second major, the PGA Championship. The next year, he won nine times and became the first man since Ben Hogan to win three majors in a single season. The following April, he won the Masters, becoming the first man in the history of the professional game to hold all four major championship trophies at the same time—the Tiger Slam, something we might never see again (unless Tiger does it).

I never saw a person strike the ball as well as Tiger did in 1999, 2000, and early 2001. At the Open Championship at St. Andrews in 2000, where he set his third major championship scoring record, I saw the greatest ball-striking exhibition I've ever seen, and perhaps the greatest in history. Tiger knows he played great golf during that time as well, but he wasn't as awestruck by his own performance as I and others who saw it were. He told me later that he remembers hitting only one "perfect" golf shot in 2000, a year where he won twelve times around the world. It was a three-wood on the fourteenth hole of the Old Course during the Open Championship, a shot he carried 260 yards to well-guarded green. He hit a perfect shot that stopped a few feet from the flag and won the tournament in record fashion—but I thought he hit a lot of "perfect" shots that week, not to mention throughout the year.

That is the attitude of an impatient perfectionist. Mr. Hogan once claimed that in his best weeks of golf he hit only three or four perfect golf shots. Tiger said he hit only one perfect shot in a year unlike any seen in the modern era of professional golf.

I have signed pin flags from Tiger's four consecutive major championships on the wall in my Las Vegas studio—mementos I'm as proud of as anything I've ever owned. It took a lot of courage for Tiger to make the changes he made at the time he made them; it took a lot of faith for him to trust the things I told him during that period; and it took a decided amount of impatience for him to work as long and hard as he did to put those changes in place. Faith and trust are the traits of a mature player and a thoughtful man: impatience is the mark of a true innovator, someone who refuses to wait on the world to take shape around him.

It took me five decades to learn those facts of life. The fact that Tiger embraced them so completely at such an early age reinforced the respect and admiration I had for the man. He won the Masters and the U.S. Open again in 2002, and finished second in the PGA Championship. That run, from January 1999 through August 2002, was, unquestionably, the most impressive streak in the history of the game.

Whenever I need a reminder of what it was like to work with Tiger, I don't have to go far. I still have most of the tapes from our practice sessions downloaded onto the computer at my Las Vegas teaching center. One particular clip, one I show to a lot of my students, demonstrates the kind of impatient competitor Tiger is. He is hitting drivers from the mats out the doors and down the range at our Las Vegas facility. I have cameras set up on all the walls as well as the ceiling so we can analyze the swings from every conceivable angle. The clip I love shows Tiger, after blowing his third shot in a row fifteen yards right of his target, hurling his driver out the door with a sidearm toss that would make Randy Johnson proud.

The camera doesn't catch it, but the club landed thirty yards downrange.

What I did get on tape a few moments later was Wayne Gretzky sticking his head around the corner and saying, "Have you ever thought about taking up tennis?" To which Tiger said, "Have you ever thought about sticking it to yourself?"

He had no patience for hitting it badly, even in practice, and he had even less patience for mistakes during competitive rounds. When he won his first U.S. Open at Pebble Beach, the only poor shot he hit all week was his second-round tee shot at the par-five eighteenth. It was Saturday morning (the second round had been delayed by fog), and Tiger hooked his tee shot into the ocean. Before the ball splashed, Tiger slammed his driver into the turf and called himself a "prick," a less than kid-friendly thing to say on national television on a Saturday morning, and an outburst he quickly apologized for. The next week the managing editor at *Golf World* magazine made up a special cover, one with a photo of Tiger slamming the driver into the ground. The headline on the cover reads: "Prick Wins U.S. Open." Only two copies of that "special issue" exist. Both are owned by Tiger.

It's easy to criticize Tiger for his occasional outbursts, just as it's easy for some people to laugh about them after the fact. What is unquestionable, however, is that the outbursts, good or bad, stem directly from his lack of patience, the same lack of patience that led him to become one of the best players in history.

All the greats share a similar aversion to patience when it comes to getting better. When Tiger was on his incredible run from 1999 through 2001, he was the best player on the PGA Tour; Hale Irwin, the winningest player in Senior Tour history, was the best player on the Senior Tour; and Annika Sorenstam was the best player on the LPGA Tour. Not one of them could be accused of being patient. David Leadbetter said that Nick Faldo was constantly pumping him for new information, wanting to learn more today than he knew yesterday and sure that he will know more tomorrow than he knows today. Arnold Palmer at age seventy-six is still impatient when it comes to his golf game. He still works on the fundamentals and has no desire to accept the inevitable declines that come with age. So don't be fooled the next time you hear a golfer tell an interviewer how he "just tried to stay patient out there." He's trying to convince himself more than you. Dad was right. All of the great ones view patience as an overrated virtue.

CLAUDE'S PEARLS

- Don't confuse playing smart with playing patient. One has absolutely nothing to do with the other.

- The best in the world are not walking around the course in a self-absorbed fog. They want to know where they stand, and they want to do whatever it takes to get to the top of the leaderboard.

- Show me someone who is obsessed with being "patient," and I'll show you someone who doesn't have the fire to be the best.

- If you don't want the answer to your question right now, and you aren't willing to do whatever it takes to find it, you'd better ask yourself: "Do I really want to know it after all?"

- If a student is willing to learn and do what is necessary to get better, you should be ready to teach him.

Eight

"You Can't Teach Talent, but You Can Sure Screw It Up"

Dad was a master at spotting potential. Ten minutes on the lesson tee and my father could size up a player's athleticism, aptitude, coordination, and temperament. He could also tell you whether or not the player had a chance at breaking a hundred, ninety, eighty, par, or becoming something special. This was more than being able to analyze a golf swing. At any PGA Tour event, the average spectator would be hard pressed to stand on the range and pick the top fifty golfers in the world based solely on the golf swings. I doubt Jim Furyk was pegged as a future U.S. Open champion when he was in college. On the other hand, Gary Nicklaus (son of Jack), Wayne Player (son of Gary), and Robert Floyd (son of Raymond), were all picked as "can't miss" future champions. They are all fine golfers and great people, but they haven't lived up to the expectations others had for them in their junior days, just as Jim Furyk surprised a lot of people with his success.

Dad had the unique ability to sort through the clutter and

pick winners from the pile. On those occasions when he found a potential champion, Dad spent an inordinate amount of time with the student. He would ask dozens of questions, listen to what the player said, and watch his mannerisms as much as his swing. He wouldn't give much advice in the early going, especially if the talented player was young. He would ask things like, "What are you thinking about before you hit this shot?" or "What are you trying to get the ball to do?"

Dad took this approach with players like a young man from Stamford, Connecticut, who joined Winged Foot as a junior member. Dad took his time with this particular student, asking many questions and giving advice sparingly. He kept close tabs on the student's practice sessions, making sure the kid didn't ingrain any bad habits. Dad would walk out onto the range in the morning and give him two or three sentences of advice. Then he would watch him take a few swings before heading back into the shop. An hour later Dad would head back to the tee and watch a few more swings, sometimes adding a comment and sometimes remaining silent. Then he would head back inside and repeat the process every hour for the rest of the day. That young man joined the tour in 1950 and in 1957 won the U.S. Open and the Tam O'Shanter World Open, and was undefeated in Ryder Cup play. His name was Dick Meyer.

Every lesson Dad gave was always specific to the student, but I noticed that his methodology changed when he was dealing with a player like Dick, or Dave Marr, or any of his sons. His advice was always sparing with us and his lessons consisted of more caregiving than speech giving. He would ask a couple of questions, make a comment or two, and spend the rest of the lesson standing nearby and occasionally saying "good" or "not quite."

One day I asked him why he seemed to have a different method for teaching certain players.

"You can't teach talent," he told me. "It's a gift from the Good Lord. You've either got it or you don't. But as a teacher, you can sure screw it up. When I see a player with real potential, I take the Hippocratic approach: my first priority is to do no harm."

At the time I shrugged and went back to whatever I was doing. It wasn't until many years later that I realized the powerful wisdom my father had packed into that answer. Ruined potential and wasted talent have become so common that they are a cliché. Every reader of this book personally knows or knows of a great young athlete, student, or artist who either wasted his gifts or was soured by an overbearing parent or an ignorant and egomaniacal coach.

Ever heard of Jack Larkin? Unless you're a golf nut with an encyclopedic knowledge of the game, you probably haven't, even though Jack was once the top-ranked junior player in the country and winner of the U.S. Boys Junior Championship. He was a good-looking, well-spoken kid with talent to burn. Jack hit the ball so straight that every iron looked like it was going in the hole. Then someone told him he needed to get longer in order to have a chance on tour. For several years, Jack tried to increase his club-head speed and hit the ball farther.

Unfortunately, clubhead speed in golf is like foot speed for a sprinter or velocity on a pitcher's fastball: you can get a little faster through hard work, but you're born with most of what you're going to get. Corey Pavin could have worked out in the gym eight hours a day for twenty years and never had the clubhead speed of John Daly, who doesn't lift anything heavier than a Marlboro and a Miller Lite. A high school football star who runs the forty-yard dash in 4.9 seconds might get a little faster, but he'll never have

4.3-speed, just like the college freshman with a 75 mile-per-hour fastball will never have Roger Clemens velocity on his pitches. Jack Larkin chased a phantom called clubhead speed, one he was never going to catch, and as a result he lost some of the accuracy that had made him so great. He is a successful businessman in Atlanta and a good amateur, but he's another in a long list of talented kids who were ruined by bad teaching.

Examples of talented players making bad choices or being led down the wrong path are legend. Dad recognized this and made a concerted effort to treat talented players with care.

"Be especially careful with kids," Dad told me during another discussion on the subject. "Young people will do what you *let* them do, and they'll do what you *make* them do. If you find a talented kid, don't let him think he can skate by on talent alone. Push him when he needs it, but bring him close when he needs that, too."

He might as well have been giving a parenting lesson, but in this case Dad was talking about golf. He went on to say: "The one thing you can be assured is that whatever you tell a kid to do, he's going to overdo. Tell a kid to strengthen his grip, and the next time you see him he'll have it too strong. Tell him to take the club a little more inside on the takeaway, and a couple of weeks later he'll be jerking it too far inside the line. That's why you not only have to be careful what you say, you have to follow up and stay on top of him. Tell a kid half as much and follow up twice as often. If you do that, you'll see greater progress than if you teach too much and leave him alone."

I realized just how right my father was when I started teaching young-talented players like Tiger Woods. It didn't take long for me to realize what a great job Tiger's early teachers, Rudy Duran and John Anselmo, had done in drilling the basics. Tiger's talent was evident from the time he was a year old and crawled out of his highchair to swing a cutoff club, so it would have been easy for Rudy or John to overdo it and fill the boy's head with more gobbledygook than he could ever erase. Fortunately, they were great teachers who struck the right balance among instruction, encouragement, and simply letting a kid be a kid. I don't think they get the credit they deserve, not only for what they taught Tiger but for what they didn't try to teach him.

I also admire the way Earl and Kultida raised their son. Golf was never forced on Tiger. In fact, even after Earl and Tida realized early on that their son had a special talent, they encouraged Tiger to enjoy other things and to take his time developing. Golf was a reward for making good grades and getting his homework done quickly. Earl never had to push Tiger. If anything, he had to hold him back.

By the time I arrived on the scene, Tiger was already a national phenomenon. He had been on the *Mike Douglas Show* at age two. The ABC show *20/20* had done a piece on him, ESPN kept up with his every move, and the *Orange County Register* had assigned a beat reporter to do nothing but follow him around—and the kid wasn't even out of high school! The young man needed strong male influences. He had that with Earl, a man who was only interested in doing what was right for his family. My job was to be another positive influence while we shaped his game for the eventuality of a professional career.

I think that Earl's decisions in the early stages of Tiger's career are more appreciated now than they were when he first burst onto the national scene. A lot of people wrongly assumed that Earl was a typical stage father, another Stefano Capriati, whose daughter Jennifer became the poster child for early-athlete burnout. From the outside, that was an easy conclusion to draw. Tiger had been in the media since he was a child, but nothing like he could have been if Earl had chosen to go with a full-blown public relations blitz. Even when Tiger was a young kid, Earl kept the media at arm's length and did a great job shepherding Tiger through the potential pitfalls of being a prodigy. The family turned down ten times as many interviews as they granted, and Earl made sure that his son wasn't hyped beyond his abilities.

Tiger could have played in a lot of professional events as a junior, too. He wouldn't have had any trouble getting sponsors' exemptions anywhere in the world. He was a novelty because of his talent, age, and ethnicity, and he would have been a draw for any event. But Earl said no. He knew that Tiger would not become a champion based on talent alone; he needed to learn to win. After he learned to win, he needed to learn to dominate. Only after he learned to dominate would Earl let him advance to the next level. It was a patient approach that is far too absent in parents today.

Tiger learned to win in the junior ranks in California and then as a junior on the national level. Only once during that time did he play in a PGA Tour event, the L.A. Open near his hometown, where he missed the cut. Tiger won every junior event in his home state and then won every junior event on a national level.

After Tiger demonstrated his dominance as a junior, Earl let him move into unrestricted amateur play, where Tiger became the greatest amateur in the world. But Earl allowed him to play only in the professional events he qualified for. He didn't seek out sponsors' exemptions or try to become "the show" before he was ready to win, even though he certainly could have gotten a lot of television time and upped his Q score if he'd gone out with the pros as a kid.

Earl was not a rich man. He had an officer's pension from the army and worked for McDonnell Douglas and then as a talent scout for a sports management company while raising Tiger. He raised his family in a modest home in Cypress, California, and he played golf at the navy courses in Los Alamitos. A lot of fathers would have been seduced by the money and fame that would have come from putting Tiger on display at an early age, but Earl swatted away every hint of temptation. He understood what my father meant when he said, "You can't teach talent, but you can screw it up." Like my dad, Earl Woods made sure that he first did no harm.

It's easy in hindsight to see what a great job Earl and Kultida did, but it is also easy to draw comparisons, the most frequent today being the comparison between Tiger and golf's newest phenomenon, Michelle Wie. In my view, there *is no* comparison. Tiger learned to win at every level before his father would allow him to move up. He became the greatest junior golfer in the world before Earl let him move into the amateur ranks. He became the greatest amateur in the world before Earl let him play with the pros. Then he became the greatest golfer in the world. He earned his promotions to the next level by winning. Not only did he win six consecutive USGA events (three U.S. Juniors and three U.S. Amateurs), all six of his final matches in those events went to the eighteenth hole or beyond. Then two out of the first three professional events he had a chance to win went to playoffs. In every instance, Tiger figured out a way to win. That takes more than talent; it takes a will to win and a confidence that you can execute under pressure.

Michelle Wie never won any national junior events and didn't play in more than a couple before turning pro at age sixteen. She started playing in professional events as a preteen, and by the time she was fourteen, she played almost exclusively with the pros. She won one USGA event and played her way into the final group on Sunday at a couple of majors as an amateur, but she never dominated at any level, despite having more talent than any woman in the game—maybe any woman in history.

Michelle has great natural ability, but swinging a golf club is a small part of learning to be a great golfer. When I see Michelle, I can't help but remember what my father said about how easy it is to screw up talent. She failed to hit quality shots down the stretch when she needed them, including the 2005 U.S. Women's Open, where she led at one point before tumbling down the leaderboard to finish in a tie for twenty-third. At the Sony Open in Hawaii, one of the PGA Tour events that offered her a sponsor's exemption, she three-putted from eight feet for a triple bogey on Friday and missed the cut. At the John Deere Classic, she was four under par and needed only pars to become the first female to make a cut in a men's PGA Tour event in sixty years. She dropped three shots in four holes and missed playing that weekend as well. Then she blew another golden opportunity when she fell apart on the back nine of the second round at the Casio World Open in Kochi, Japan.

Not being able to close the deal under pressure shows a lack of experience, but I have also been concerned by how mechanical her game appears to have become. You can almost see her brain reeling off the punch list of things she needs to remember as she sets up to hit a shot. There isn't the natural flow and ease of motion that was evident when she first burst onto the scene as a fourteen-year-old. I worry about her game becoming too robotic. I'm also alarmed by her ambivalent attitude toward not winning. None of the great players in history felt comfortable "progressing" in their games, and nobody who has a likeness hanging in the Hall of Fame ever felt good about making a cut or finishing in the top ten. As Tiger said during his rookie year, "Second place sucks." Every great player in history has agreed with him.

There are the rare occasions when losing is not a terrible thing, especially for a young player. I remember when Adam Scott lost to Tiger in the semifinals of the World Match Play Championship. Adam is one of the nicest, quietest, calmest guys in golf, but he was so hot after that loss that I thought he might grab the bumper of his courtesy car and flip it over in the parking lot. He had outplayed Tiger only to lose at the end. Afterward I said to Adam, "You don't believe it now, but I think this loss is the best thing that could have happened to you as a player."

Through clenched teeth he said, "Winning would have been better."

"No," I said, "Losing this one will actually do more for you than winning would have because you're so mad, you're going to work twice as hard as you've ever worked to keep it from happening again."

"I'm pretty hot."

"I know you are," I said. "You should be. You know you outplayed the best player in the world, and he knows you outplayed him. The only thing you didn't do was make the last putt. He did, and that's why he's ranked number one.

"Now, I want you to remember what this feels like; sear it in your memory so the next time you're in a position to win you'll do whatever it takes to keep from feeling this way again."

I was wrong about one thing with Adam: his loss to Tiger didn't drive him to work twice as hard; it drove him to work ten times harder. As of this writing, he is the sixth-ranked player in the world and getting better every day.

I don't see that same drive to win with Michelle Wie, in part because she hasn't won a lot and doesn't understand how important it is. Tiger didn't have that problem. Winning on the PGA Tour came naturally to him because he'd won everywhere he'd played. The tour was a natural progression. Michelle has been trotted out like a pregame carnival act, and when she has put up a couple of decent numbers, she has smiled, waved, and been content to sign autographs and give interviews.

She also is making a terrible mistake by continuing to play with the men, where she has no chance of winning. Not only does the sort of drubbing she's taking on the PGA Tour begin to wear you down, it is also a slap in the face of the LPGA Tour, a great organization that is more popular today than the Champions Tour and the Nationwide Tour. Michelle could be the shining star in a rising league, but not if she insists on competing in events she has no chance of winning and fails to win those events where she could have a great impact on the game.

That is not to say that she won't learn to win soon. She just hasn't learned to yet, and the arena in which she now competes makes that learning curve a lot steeper.

Comparisons between Michelle and Tiger are natural, but unfair. A fairer comparison for Michelle would be Paula Creamer in her rookie year (at age nineteen). Paula won twice on the LPGA Tour in her first year and was the hero of the 2005 Solheim Cup.

She developed legions of fans with her pink clothes and her charming smiles. She showed the kind of gritty competitiveness that serious sportsmen love to watch and the kind of unfiltered emotion that send advertisers scrambling for their checkbooks. She proved herself inside the ropes and has been a tremendous asset for the LPGA Tour outside the ropes. That same year, Michelle failed to win anything and missed the cuts in all of her men's professional tour appearances. Still, Michelle received a reported $10 million in endorsements by turning pro the same week she turned sixteen.

No one faults a family for making money. But I've always gotten the sense that Michelle missed out on being a teenager—something she will probably never be able to recapture. When she missed the cut at the John Deere, ten thousand people had followed her around the course. The tournament's gross receipts were up 40 percent from the previous year (without Michelle), and the television ratings spiked by 54 percent. More than two million people watched her on TV. Three times that number watched her giggle and joke with David Letterman the week after she turned pro.

She also appeared on the cover of *Fortune* magazine, which devoted eleven pages to Michelle and ran an alluring black-and-white photo of her under the headline "Wie Will Rock You." The magazine also hailed her as a "sweet sixteen marketing machine."

In my opinion, that's the problem. Michelle's press conference the day she turned pro made me cringe, not because of her golf abilities but because of her age and the fact that I felt she was being exploited by the adults in her life. And I was not alone in that opinion. Uncomfortable questions started bubbling to the surface not long after Michelle's camp announced her intentions. The most disquieting among them was, "Why now? She's only sixteen." The answer might have been money, and if so, it's hard to fault her parents. But parents of children who worked in sweatshops at the turn of the last century needed money, too. That didn't stop responsible adults from passing child labor laws. With Michelle, the public has let her golf ability, her charm, and her uniqueness cloud the fact that she will not be able to vote until 2008; and she will not be able to rent a car or buy a drink until the fall of 2010, five years after making her professional debut.

I hope she does well. I hope Michelle wins decisively and becomes a star on the LPGA Tour, and I hope she grows to become a well-balanced, stable, mature woman. Only time will tell. But I believe the adults in her life have done her a grave disservice. Not only have her parents pushed her to play at the highest level before her experience and maturity justified it, the other adults surrounding her have, in my opinion, put inordinate pressure on a sixteen-year-old little girl by holding her out as the next great phenom, by setting the expectations bar impossibly high.

Rehab clinics and therapists' offices are filled with former child actors, past-their-prime tennis stars, and once prepubescent pop singers who never had childhoods and who struggle to cope as adults. I hope Michelle Wie is not headed down that path. Nothing in her demeanor suggests such an outcome, and I, like most, hope for the best. I also hope I'm proved wrong and her parents did the right thing. But one thing is for certain: there is no doubt that Earl Woods did the right thing when he raised Tiger. I just hope Michelle's talent is strong enough to propel her over the hurdles that have been erected in her path.

Tiger's hurdles when he was sixteen were no different from those of any other high school kid. He wanted the best-looking girlfriend, he wanted the kids in school to think he was cool, even though he was skinny and wore glasses, and he wanted to win every tournament he entered. On one of those three counts, Tiger had no problem.

The only problem I had with Tiger was the same one I'd seen my father have when he was teaching motivated young people. If I wanted Tiger to get the club slightly more outside on his takeaway, he would work on it at a frantic pace until it was too far outside. If I asked him to get a little closer to the ball at address, the next time I saw him he would be crowding the ball and having to clear his hips quickly to make contact. Whatever I asked him to do I could rest assured he was going to overdo.

So, I did with Tiger what I saw my dad do with the kids he taught: I said little and watched a lot.

Like all talented people, Tiger Woods also had a stubborn streak. There were certain aspects of the game where he made up his mind and no one could change it. Most of the time he was open and receptive to anything I said, but there were occasions when I ran headlong into the Stubborn Tiger. On those occasions, I simply had to accept that this was the price you paid for dealing with someone who possessed extraordinary skills.

For example, in the first weeks of January 1998, while Tiger was still in his early twenties and he and I were in the middle of his controversial swing changes, I walked onto the range at La Costa in Carlsbad, California, during the Mercedes Championships, holding a new Cobra driver with a prototype shaft from A.J. Tech. The bright red shaft had the grip molded onto the end so that it was seamless with the shaft. Tiger saw the club and said, "What's that?"

I explained the concept, and he said, "Let me hit it."

"No, it's not made for you. The shaft's not stiff enough."

He insisted, so I handed over the driver. Tiger teed up a ball and flew his first shot more than three hundred and forty yards, through the back of the range. His second shot flew even farther.

"You know, I can have them put one of those shafts in your driver," I said.

"No," he said. "I can't control a graphite shaft. Maybe I'll get one to play with at home so I can hit it a hundred yards past my buddies."

He had just hit two perfect drives well over three hundred yards with a prototype graphite shaft. I felt certain he could have stood out there all day and never hit the shot more than five or ten yards off line. At the time Tiger hit a steel-shafted driver that was a half-inch shorter than standard. He felt the shorter, heavier shaft gave him more control. I could have argued the point. I thought he could hit a graphite shaft and be just as accurate while gaining another fifteen to twenty yards on his tee shots, but I knew he would disagree. We'd been over it before. This was a blind spot for him at the time, so I let it go.

Today, Tiger hits a graphite-shafted driver and is always near the top of the statistics charts in overall driving.

I thought of Dad a lot when I was on the range with Tiger, especially when I would go long periods of time without saying a word. "Teaching a talented winner is like riding a thoroughbred racehorse," Dad would say. "The horse knows how to run. You've just got to keep him running in the right direction."

I did my part to keep Tiger between the fence lines. Not only did we do some great work on the golf course together, I felt like I helped him deal with the growing pains of being the most watched golfer in history and one of the most recognized athletes on the planet. In fact, the part of our relationship I'm proudest of was the lessons I helped Tiger with off the course.

When Tiger was a rookie, for example, he said things like, "I proved today I could win with my C game." After he made that statement I pulled him aside and said, "I know what you meant, and you know what you meant, but that's not how it's going to sound on the news. You don't ever want to say anything that can be misconstrued as disrespectful to the other players. I know that wasn't your intention, but that's the way it's going to play."

Dad was never that subtle with my brothers or me. "If you don't open your mouth, only half the world thinks you're an idiot," Dad would say to me after I'd made some bone-headed comment. "But when you open your mouth, you remove any doubts the other half might have had."

I also counseled Tiger through some petulant moments, which were rare and mild compared to some of the things I did when I was playing. As I've said, I broke clubs, swore, and made a jackass of myself more often than I care to remember. About the worst thing Tiger did as a rookie was refuse to talk to the media after a bad opening round in his first U.S. Open as a pro, even though a podium had been set up so that he did not have to go out of his way. When he ignored the waiting press and stormed off, he spent most of the next day explaining why he'd blown everybody off.

"You're never going to win that battle," I told him. "When you're crawling into bed and turning out the lights, they [the media] are going to be writing their stories. More people are going to read what they write than hear your rebuttal. Looking at this one incident, you spent more time and more words explaining why you walked away than you would have spent taking a couple of questions immediately after the round."

He learned quickly. By the time he started his second full year on tour, Tiger was as media savvy as any player in the game, and one of the most liked and admired players among his peers.

I got to be part of the team that helped a kid grow into a man, a fact I'm probably more proud of than the records we amassed together. I also got to be there for some of the funnier moments of the process, too. Shortly after he turned pro, I traveled with Tiger to San Antonio for another of the events on his sponsor's exemption tour. During the flight I said, "You know, Tig, you need to get some decent clothes. Everything you own has the Nike swoosh on it. That's fine for the golf course, but you can't go out to dinner with swooshes all over you."

To my shock, he agreed to let me take him shopping when we landed. I found the best men's store in San Antonio, took him in, and introduced him to silk shirts and cashmere sweaters. He had a blast. The owner recognized him, so he signed autographs and posed for pictures as we shopped.

When we got ready to leave, he pulled out one of the new credit cards IMG, his management company, had gotten for him and tossed it on the counter. The clerk ran it, and with an embarrassed look came back to us and said, "Mr. Woods, I'm sorry, this card was rejected."

Tiger didn't know what to do, so I said, "You know, the guy is Tiger Woods. Try it one more time."

Same result.

"That's strange," Tiger said as he pulled out anther card.

"I'm sorry, Mr. Woods," he said. "That one's also rejected."

Two more cards, and two more rejections later, I picked up the tab for the clothes, about two grand, if my memory is correct. As we were in the car on the way back to the hotel, Tiger said, "That is so weird about those cards. They're brand-new."

That's when it dawned on me. "Tiger, you did activate those cards, didn't you?"

"What do you mean?"

"That white strip on the back with the eight-hundred number—you did call, didn't you?"

"No, I just threw that away."

He learned a lot in those first few months, just as I learned a lot about carefully handing the combination of youth and talent.

I think Dad would have been proud of how I handled my time with Tiger. I know I am.

CLAUDE'S PEARLS

- Talent can't be taught. God's either blessed you with certain gifts or He hasn't, and no amount of work will change that.

- As a parent and a coach, you have to recognize what talents a kid does or does not have. Don't pressure a kid to try to do things he cannot do.

- Kids are going to do what you let them do and what you make them do. Make sure you understand that balance.

- When you find someone who has talent, be careful: while you can't teach certain skills, you can certainly screw them up. The first rule of dealing with talented people is "Do no harm."

- The most successful formula for teaching talented young people is to say less and be there more. Your presence is more important than your words.

Nine

"Take Care of the People You Meet, and They Will Take Care of You"

Dad was one of the most giving people in the world, and everyone loved him for it. He would give you his last dollar (and often did) for no other reason than he thought you needed it more than he did. I remember one caddy at Winged Foot named Racket, who used to hit Dad up for money on a daily basis. His standard line was, "Hey, Pro, how 'bout giving me two. I need to go see Sue," and Dad would reach into his pocket and give him cash. I never understood it. With his sons and with himself, Dad was a huge proponent of earning your own way. He never accepted charity and never allowed us to ever consider it. When a great family friend named Jack Mulcahy bought three lots in Palm Desert and tried to give Dad a house, Dad wouldn't take it. "I worked too hard for the one we've got," he said. But every day he would give Racket money. Finally, after watching Dad dole out another handful of bills to Racket, Billy was standing outside the caddy pen when Racket said to him, "You know something, boy? I knew your daddy's momma."

That night when Billy asked Dad about it, Dad said, "He's right. Racket grew up in Georgia, and he knew my mother."

"Is that why you give him money all the time?" Billy asked.

Dad thought for a second, and said, "No. I keep him around because of that. I give him money because he needs it."

One of Dad's great joys in life was taking care of people. "If you take care of everybody you meet, they will eventually take care of you," he said. "Don't be a taker, always be a giver. And don't be like all the other golf pros in the world. They're the cheapest people who ever lived. If you go out to dinner with a group of members who are good customers, pick up the tab. Don't expect the members to pay just because they're members or because they might have more money than you. That's what takers do. If you take all the time, people will eventually stop giving."

A great example of that philosophy was a habit Dad had when he played tour events in the forties. At every stop, Dad would write a note to the club member who let Dad use his locker for the week. Rarely, if ever, did he meet the guys. But every week he would leave a little handwritten "thank you" in the locker, along with a glove or a sleeve or two of balls. It was a classy touch, one a lot of today's tour players could learn from. Years later, when he was interviewing for the professional job at Thunderbird, a member of the selection committee named Walter Cruttenden spoke up toward the end of the interview. "I want you all to know that when we lived in Chicago, the tour would come to town for the Western Open, a big tournament in those days, and I would always give up my locker to a tour pro," he said. "In all those years Claude Harmon was the only pro to leave me a 'thank you' note. He also left a sleeve of balls."

Dad had never met Mr. Cruttenden before, and he hadn't played in Chicago in a decade, but he knew at that moment that he was a lock for the job at Thunderbird. A random act of courtesy and kindness had come full circle.

"Give what you've got to others," he would say. "It doesn't have to be money. Give a tip to a friend who's struggling with his game. Go out of your way to visit somebody who might not be having the best year. And always be nice to every person you meet. It doesn't cost a dime to be nice and polite, and the dividends will come back to you in ways you can't imagine. But if you're a prick, word spreads, and you'll be known as a prick for the rest of your life."

Dad had seen how people's perceptions could come back to haunt you. He had witnessed it with his friend, Ben Hogan. Mr. Hogan was one of the most misunderstood men in the game, in part because people simply could not accept the fact that he was an introverted person who had exacting standards for himself and those around him. When he would dismiss or ignore a reporter who asked a stupid question, he was labeled as rude and aloof, when in fact he was simply trying to elevate the dialogue between reporters and the subjects they covered. When he failed to acknowledge the crowds, it was not because he didn't like people; it was because he was so focused he didn't see them. He didn't even notice his wife when she went out on the course to watch him. Because of these traits, Mr. Hogan is the only player in history with whom the word *mystique* is universally associated. In contrast, we thought he was one of the most delightful and courteous people we'd ever met.

When he visited our home, or when we would see him out on tour, Mr. Hogan went out of his way to ask each of us how we were doing. He wanted to know how we were faring in school and how our golf games were progressing. These were not courtesy questions; he was genuinely interested in our well-being. Of course, like everyone else in the fifties, we were awestruck by the "Hogan mystique," even though we knew Mr. Hogan as one of Dad's best friends in the game. I believe they were close because Mr. Hogan admired the way Dad lived his life and how he had sacrificed a promising career on tour to support his family by taking a club job. I also think he secretly wished he could be a little bit more like my father. Dad and Mom had six children. Mr. Hogan and Valerie had none, even though Mr. Hogan loved kids and doted over his nieces. Dad was a breezy conversationalist, a guy who was at ease in any and all social settings and who could have a crowd in stitches within five minutes of entering a room. Mr. Hogan never felt comfortable chitchatting, and he was more likely to combust spontaneously than to play a casual round of golf with a high-handicap member. I know my father admired Mr. Hogan for his dedicated work ethic and the near perfection he achieved on the golf course, as well as the way he had pulled himself up from nothing to become the greatest golfer in the world. In many ways, I think they were envious of each other, while remaining the best of friends.

Every year some golf reporter rewrites the story of Dad and Mr. Hogan playing together in the 1947 Masters. When they came to the par-three twelfth, Mr. Hogan hit first, a perfect shot right over the flag, leaving himself a downhill three-footer. Dad then hit a shot that never left the flag. It bounced once, rattled the flagstick, and fell in for a hole-in-one. The crowd, such as it was back then, went wild. Dad hugged his caddy, waved to the gallery, and then trotted across the little bridge over Rae's Creek, snatched the ball out of the hole, and waved again. Mr. Hogan then made his putt for birdie.

As they walked to the thirteenth tee, Mr. Hogan said, "You know, Claude, I think that's the first time I've ever birdied that hole . . . What did you have?"

Dad knew him well enough not to be surprised. "I had a one, Ben," was all he said. Ben just nodded, and wrote a one down on the scorecard.

Dad was the only player Mr. Hogan would go to for swing advice, and Dad and Jimmy Demaret were the only players close enough to Mr. Hogan to offer any unsolicited tips. During one of their practice rounds at Augusta National in 1952, the year before Mr. Hogan's record-setting triple-crown season, Dad noticed a problem with Mr. Hogan's putting, one that stemmed from the most talked-about automobile accident of the last half-century.

On Groundhog Day, February 2, 1949, Mr. Hogan was almost killed on Highway 80 east of Van Horn, Texas, when a Greyhound bus crossed the centerline of the icy highway and slammed head-on into his Cadillac. The only thing that saved Mr. Hogan's life was the fact that he had slowed his car to a practical stop because of the hazardous conditions. Seeing the bus and knowing what was about to happen, he threw his body onto the passenger side to shield his ninety-eight-pound wife, Valerie.

Most historians have focused on the impact this famous car crash had on Mr. Hogan's legs. That was the central theme of the movie *Follow the Sun*, starring Glenn Ford as Mr. Hogan in the dramatic tale of the comeback after doctors told Mr. Hogan he might never walk again. He confided in Dad (and no one else) that the accident also restricted his hip turn and probably cost him ten yards of distance off the tee. He also told Dad and few others that the crash almost blinded him in his left eye. He was already forty years old, so his eyesight wasn't what it had been twenty years before, but the effects of the crash caused him to lose most of his depth perception. He couldn't pick up the subtle breaks in the greens the way he once could, and he had a hard time gauging distance.

For the rest of his career, Mr. Hogan would stand over putts forever. Some said he "froze" over three-footers. In fact, he was simply trying to adjust his eyesight before he pulled the trigger. Sometimes he was successful; often he was not. Dad saw the frustrations Mr. Hogan was having on the greens, so as they walked off the eighteenth green at Augusta National, Dad put his arm around his friend and said, "Ben, I can help you with your putting if you'll let me. What do you say?"

Mr. Hogan looked at the ground and said, "What do *you* say?"

"Come to the practice green and let me show you."

Mr. Hogan said, "No, show me right here."

That was tough since they were standing between the eighteenth green and the first tee, only a few feet from the practice green. Dad showed Mr. Hogan how his right-hand grip pressure was too tight, which caused the right hand to overpower the left during the stroke. This resulted in the left wrist breaking during impact—the kiss of death on greens as fast as Augusta National's.

I can't say if Dad's tip helped. Mr. Hogan didn't win the Masters that year, and he didn't win a single major in 1952. But the very fact that Mr. Hogan listened to Dad's advice was a testament to their friendship and the respect each man had for the other.

Mr. Hogan trusted Dad's eye when it came to the subtleties and nuances of the professional game, but he would also listen to Dad on other matters. After the crash, Dad was one of the first to phone the hospital to check on Mr. Hogan's condition. He stayed in touch with Valerie every day during that period, and he offered, more than once, to leave Florida and fly to Texas to be at his friend's bedside. Had there been anything he could have done, there's no question Dad would have been there. He was there for sure when Mr. Hogan made his comeback in Philadelphia, winning the U.S. Open at Merion a little more than a year after the crash that was supposed to leave him crippled for life. My father was one of the first competitors to congratulate Mr. Hogan after that win. And he was one of the only pros to line the parade route in Manhattan on Ben Hogan Day for the tickertape parade after Mr. Hogan became the only man in history to win the Masters, the U.S. Open, and the British Open in the same season. They talked about politics, faith, business, sports, and the future of golf. They were the kinds of conversations you would expect from lifetime friends, even those who were as seemingly different as Mr. Hogan and my dad.

When it came to golf, Mr. Hogan was not immune from giving Dad advice, either. Seven years after Dad offered Mr. Hogan his putting tip after their practice round at Augusta, Mr. Hogan offered my father a tip on how to win the 1959 U.S. Open at Winged Foot. "Now, Claude," he said, "you should win this golf tournament. Nobody knows this golf course better than you, and nobody can play it as well as you. Nobody else should win. I'm going to tell you how to do it: You need to forget those members for the week. Pretend they don't exist. When you arrive at the club, walk with your head down and don't speak to anybody. No 'How are you, Mrs. Harvey?' or 'Did you get your tickets okay, Mr. Smith?' Go straight into the locker room without speaking to a soul. And don't even think about going into the golf shop to check on sales. If you want to eat, eat by yourself. When you're finished with your round, go straight to the range without saying a word, and when you've got all your work done, put your head down and head straight for your car. If you do that, you'll win this golf tournament. But you won't. You can't. You're a jolly golfer. That's why you won't win."

Dad almost won. He finished third to Billy Casper, and ahead of Mr. Hogan. He would have won had he not putted miserably the entire week. Still, third place in the U.S. Open was the best finish by a club pro in the modern era, a feat not likely to be equaled.

I was lucky to spend a lot of time with Dad and all of his friends, including Mr. Hogan, on and off the golf course. When we were in the car once on our way to another major, I asked Dad, "Is Mr. Hogan your friend?"

He nodded, but didn't make eye contact with me, which was unusual. When Dad was making a point, he looked at you. This time, he looked away, which I didn't understand at the time. "He is a good friend," he said, staring out the window at something on the horizon that I couldn't see.

"Seems odd," I said.

"What does?"

"Mr. Hogan doesn't seem like the kind of fellow who has a lot of friends," I said.

Dad shook his head and said, "You don't need a lot of friends. A few good ones are more than most men could ask for. Friendships take work. They don't just grow in the air like bacteria. Mr. Hogan and I are friends because we work at being friends. It's that simple."

Mr. Hogan remained Dad's friend throughout his life. Anytime the Hogans were in New York, he and Valerie would come to my parents' home, and anytime I was in Fort Worth, I would make it a point to stop by his office and say hello. Invariably, Mr. Hogan would take me out to lunch or dinner, where he would share incredible stories about his days on tour and the good times he shared with my father. Dad would grow irritated when newspaper reporters would write that Mr. Hogan was "arrogant" or, worse, "rude." The man Dad knew, the man who loved children and dogs, who cried uncontrollably when a stray dog was killed near his club in Fort Worth, who made more anonymous contributions to people in need than anyone Dad had ever seen, who loved to dance, and the man my father would call "friend" for his entire adult life, didn't show himself to many people. There is never a question in my mind that if I had needed anything at all, I could have called Mr. Hogan. He was one of the people my father had in mind when he told us to keep our friends close. "Always take care of people," Dad would say. "Someday you might need to be taken care of yourself. How you've treated others in your life will most likely reflect how you're treated when you need help."

Dad had many friends, in part because he was the kind of person you wanted to be around, the "jolly golfer," as Mr. Hogan called him. People warmed to him quickly and worked at cultivating his friendship. This was not for personal gain; many of Dad's friends had more material wealth than Dad had ever dreamed possible. Dad knew that true friendships cut through the material and superficial, and they go to the heart of what kind of man you are. He never tried to befriend someone because of that person's job or station in life. "A friend is your friend when you're up and when you're down," he would say. "If you don't return a friend's call when he needs you, you don't deserve his friendship or anybody else's, for that matter."

That was the way he approached all his relationships, and it was one of the reasons he always had plenty of friends. One such friendship my father cultivated over the years led to a major turning point in my life and career.

When I was working with Greg Norman, a lot of reporters asked me if Greg's toys impressed me. He always had the biggest boat, the fastest sports cars, the best jet; it was easy to see how someone could have been in awe. In fact, I think many of the reporters were awed themselves, which is what prompted them to ask the question in the first place. But I told them, "No, the stuff is nice, but I'm not particularly impressed."

"How can you not be impressed?" one of them asked.

I smiled and said, "Hey, I've worked for a guy who has his picture on his country's money while he's still alive. Now, that's impressive."

I was referring to His Royal Majesty, King Hassan II, the King of Morocco, whom I worked for as the Royal Golf Instructor for the better part of ten years. His Majesty was also the man who had more influence on my life than anyone other than my father.

I worked for the King because of Dad, who started working for him because of Tommy Armour. His Majesty's physician had recommended that he take up golf because tennis was putting too much pressure on his load-bearing joints. Knowing nothing about the game, the King read the French translation of Mr. Armour's instructional book *How to Play Your Best Golf.* The King loved it so much he extended an invitation to Tommy to come to Morocco. Tommy used to always joke that he had no idea where Morocco was, and when he found out he decided he couldn't make it. The truth was that Mr. Armour's own health was not the greatest, and he couldn't travel. What he did instead was suggest that His Majesty contact Dad.

Dad wanted to go to Morocco, but he wasn't sure Winged Foot would give him the time off to travel to Rabat. Fortunately, the U.S. Department of State stepped in on his behalf; at the request of the Moroccan ambassador, they officially requested that Claude Harmon be given a ten-day leave of absence in the middle of the golf season to travel to Morocco. The club's board granted the request, and Dad and Mom flew to Morocco in 1968 for a ten-day, one-on-one clinic with the King.

His Majesty hit balls from beneath a large tent, since the Moroccan sun makes hitting balls in the open air for any length of time virtually impossible. But Dad had trouble following the flight of the ball once it left the tent, so he said, "Your Majesty, in order to teach you, I have to be able to see what the ball's doing in the air. I'm having trouble doing that from under this tent." Twenty-four hours later, a new forty-foot-high tent was in place. Dad didn't have any trouble following the ball flight after that.

When the ten days were up, His Majesty asked Dad and Mom to stay full time. Dad told him that he had to return to Winged Foot, but that he would make periodic visits to check on the King's progress. He paid more than sixty visits to Morocco after that.

The King even came to Winged Foot while in town for the United Nations conference. Secret Service agents swarmed the club prior to his arrival. They searched every room in the clubhouse and set up several observation posts on the grounds. With tensions between Muslims and Jews running high, there was big concern about the proximity of Winged Foot to Quaker Ridge, the best Jewish club in Westchester County, located no more than a seven-iron shot from the back edge of the Winged Foot property. Certainly the members at Quaker Ridge had no beef with His Majesty, and I know the King would have had no problem with them, but you never know when somebody will try to stir up trouble, so the Secret Service put extra security around the fence line. Security guards also communicated His Majesty's every move to the men on the ground, which was hilarious. The caddy master, Pat Collins, heard one agent announce, "He's in the elevator."

"What elevator?" Pat asked, assuming he had somehow missed the King's arrival.

"The service elevator."

"Here?"

"No, at the Waldorf-Astoria."

When His Majesty finally arrived, the caravan of limos stretched around the front entry circle and down the driveway the entire length of the driving range. After His Majesty changed into golf attire and got to the first tee, there were at least a hundred members of a joint American-Moroccan delegation there to watch him tee off. Luckily, the King had gotten pretty good by then. He was a very athletic man, a world-class horseman and expert rifleman, so he picked up the basics pretty quickly. He struggled with his putting and fought a slice because he tended to hang back on his right side through impact, but he never felt intimidated by a crowd, which was a good thing since he never played without one.

At Winged Foot, he had twenty potential playing partners

lined up with clubs in hand on the first tee. They showed up with pull carts, but Pat Collins confiscated those and almost caused an international incident. When His Majesty arrived on the tee, he looked up and down the line of players like a beauty pageant judge. Then he pointed at two men and said, "You and you." The men joined the King and Dad, and the rest trotted off to the parking lot.

The King could not have been kinder to my father, and they became close friends. When Dad contracted a bone infection in his left wrist, the King insisted on flying him to Paris to see a specialist. The doctor removed three inches of bone from my father's ulna, which probably saved his life. But when Dad got home and had to have the stitches removed, the King insisted that he fly back to Paris.

"Thank you, Your Majesty," Dad said, "but I can get stitches out at Eisenhower Medical Center [in Palm Springs], which is two miles up the road."

The King was having none of it, and by nightfall, Dad had a first-class ticket on Royal Air Morocco to Paris.

Dad continued to travel to Morocco until his health no longer allowed it. During one of his trips, he found himself in the middle of a coup attempt where he was lucky to escape with his life. It was July 1971, nine months after Mom died, and Dad was at the palace for the King's annual birthday bash. The festivities included a military review; when gunfire and explosions erupted, a few of the guests thought they were being treated to a mock battle exercise. The appearance of blood, however, made everyone realize that this was not a drill. Several of the guests were shot to death on the palace lawn. Dad and famous golf course architect Robert Trent Jones Sr., were herded at gunpoint to a road near the golf course, where they found themselves side by side, lying face-down, after being hit in the back with the rifle butts. Mr. Jones was lying on Dad's left. The man on his right, whom Dad did not know, said something to the soldiers in Arabic. He was shot in the head. Blood and bone splattered all over Dad, but he didn't move, even after being kicked repeatedly in the legs and neck.

Four hours into the ordeal, someone reported that the King had escaped. The rebels abandoned the palace and its remaining guests. Two days later, the uprising was quashed, but not before six hundred people had been killed. Dad felt very fortunate not to have been one of them. He told stories about being present for the coup attempt for the rest of his life.

Robert Trent Jones, who had helped Bobby Jones (no relation) tinker with Augusta National during the fifties and sixties, was present for the attempted coup because Dad had recommended him to the King when His Majesty set out to build a championship golf course ten miles outside of Rabat. The result was Royal Golf Dar es Salaam, a 7,508-yard par seventy-three course that wound through a cork forest. At the time it opened in 1971, Dar es Salaam ranked as one of the hardest golf courses in the world.

While the course was under construction, the King invited me over for the Moroccan Open. I was in my rookie year on tour at the time and had never been to North Africa, so I accepted—and actually played pretty well. During that trip, His Majesty asked me to take a look at Dar es Salaam and give my opinion. I did, and said some positive things about the course, which were all true. His Majesty listened to my comments and said, "Would you consider being our first golf professional when we open?"

I didn't think he was serious, so I said, "Sure, I'd be happy to."

I finished second in the Moroccan Open that year and never thought about the conversation again.

Two years later, in the fall of 1971, I got a call from the Moroccan embassy. The undersecretary said, "We're ready for you."

"Ready for me to what?" I asked.

"Ready for you to come."

"Come where?"

"Morocco. The golf course is ready now. You are to be our first golf professional."

My golf game wasn't paying the bills, and I liked the King. There was no better teaching job in the world that I knew of, so that afternoon I called my first wife and said, "How's your French?"

"Rusty," she said. "Why?"

"You need to brush up. We're moving to North Africa."

The King turned out to be a fantastic student and a wonderful friend to both my father and to me. It would have been easy to be intimidated by him. After all, he ran a country, lived in one of the most opulent palaces in the world, and of course, had his face on the currency. But I remembered my dad's lessons about the ball and club not caring who you were or where you lived, and that memory allowed me to relax and feel confident when I was on the lesson tee with His Majesty. Soon, we started talking about things other than golf, and within a year, I considered him to be a great friend.

Most of his golf was limited to nine holes because he didn't have time for a complete eighteen. Even then he would be interrupted three or four times to sign documents or take calls. I asked him once how he could concentrate through all the interruptions.

He shrugged and said, "I have to run my country."

This was before the days of everyone owning cellular phones, but His Majesty had one on his golf cart, and he would always take two or three calls a round. One day I was at his golf course in Fez when the power went out at my house in Rabat. As the afternoon wore on I was concerned that nightfall might come before the power was restored. When His Majesty went inside for a moment, I used the phone on his cart to call home and get an update.

The King came back out and said, "Claude [he never called me Butch], is everything all right?"

"Yes, Your Majesty," I said.

"Are you sure? Because I saw you use my phone. I know you wouldn't have done that unless something was wrong."

So I told him that the power was out at home, and with the sun going down, I was concerned about my family.

"Oh, I'm sure they will be fine," he said.

After the round I called home to get another update, and the first words out of my wife's mouth were, "What did you do?"

"I had to hang up. His Majesty came out, and . . ."

"That's not what I mean."

"What are you talking about?"

"Fifteen minutes after you called, every power truck in the city was here."

"So, do you have power?" I asked.

"Oh, yes, not only do I have power, we now have a backup generator and the home number of the head of the power company. I can call him anytime, day or night."

Such were the perks of working with royalty. I also had to be careful not to make any offhand comments. If I said something like, "I've never understood why that bunker is there," it would be gone the next morning. And if I said, "This hole would be a lot better if we had a big tree guarding the right of the green," a twenty-foot tree would be standing there within twenty-four hours. He trusted my judgment on all things golf, and I enjoyed his recommendations on many other things.

The material things the King gave me were secondary to the friendship we had and the way he treated me. My adult life had been spent in the military where hierarchy is everything, and on tour where your worth was judged by the scores you shot. The King could have treated me as an employee or a subject, and that would have been fine. The fact that he treated me as a friend is something that I value. He shared a lot of special things with me, things that will remain private for the rest of my life out of respect for him and in deference to the respect that he showed to my father and to me.

Had I not been my father's first-born son, there is no way I would ever even have met King Hassan II. It was Dad's personality and knowledge of the game that provided him the entrée to the King. It was his empathy, compassion, and willingness to be open and honest in his critiques of such an important and imposing figure that allowed them to strike up a lasting friendship.

Learning the value and nature of friendships from my father allowed me to develop one of the most important and lasting friendships of my life. And working for His Majesty gave me the personal confidence to go on to coach two players who became the top-ranked golfers in the world. For that I will always be grateful to my dad and to King Hassan II.

The most important thing a person can do in life is take care of another human being and to be a positive influence those with whom you come into contact. Often we don't realize how our actions affect those we have met along the way (both positively and negatively), nor do we always know how important other people are in our lives until it's too late.

The Harmons discovered this fact the hard way in the fall of 1970. My mother Alice was always the cement of the family, the hardening agent that held a bunch of brick-top, testosterone-cured egos together. She took care of us, kept us in line, and set an example of giving that none of her male children could ever match. When she died of cancer on November 5, 1970, at age fifty-one, the mortar of our family began to crumble.

Dad was never the same after Mom passed away. Their relationship had been a thirty-year love affair. They had been best friends, and when she was gone, Dad didn't know how to cope. She had made him a better, more civilized man. He never swore in front of any woman, but especially not in the presence of my mother, and he always stood when any female approached or left the dining table. Part of this came from his formal southern upbringing, as I've said, but a lot of it stemmed from his relationship with Mom. He always wanted to please her.

It wasn't until she was gone that we began to realize that none of us had ever heard our parents fight. Even when Dad went through his financial crisis with the Ford dealership, we never heard a raised voice. Mom stood by her man no matter what, and Dad loved her with everything he had. When she died, he fell apart. We all did.

At the time I didn't think Mom's passing affected me in any profound way, but in hindsight I realized that her death sparked the time in my life when I started drinking and gambling too much. My brother Craig retreated into a personal cocoon, becoming even more quiet and reserved than usual, and walling himself off from those who were closest to him. Dick tried to fill the void of Mom's absence by controlling everything he could and looking after everyone. Our younger sisters, Claudia and Alison, handled things better than any of the boys. They were strong, and did everything in their power to take care of Dad in Mom's absence. But Billy suffered the most. Not only did he lose his mother at a crucial time, he witnessed his father, whose validation Billy lived for, suffer through some of the most difficult years of his life. Billy turned to alcohol and drugs, and became an addict. In his own words, he felt like "the lowest piece of crap who ever lived."

Compounding things, Dad's arthritis got worse in the early seventies—so much so that he could no longer play golf, meaning he lost the two great loves of his life at the same time. Now, suddenly, he was a beaten and broken man, a shell of his former self, someone whose "care" meter was running on empty. Dad's tongue got sharper with the members at Winged Foot and Thunderbird. He began to break one of the inviolate rules he had always laid out for his assistants: he starting drinking with, and in front of, the members. Scotch was the preferred grief killer, at first with water, then on the rocks, and finally neat. When he drank, the verbal quips got a little sharper, edgier, and meaner, the wit no longer had sparkle, and he lost his ability to feel much of anything.

The members began to notice. Days before the 1974 U.S. Open at Winged Foot, several members came though the grillroom and asked Dad how many under par he thought would win. He told them that nobody would shoot under par. The members couldn't believe he'd said that. With players like Johnny Miller, Jack Nicklaus, Raymond Floyd, Hubert Green, and Hale Irwin ripping par to shreds, all the members agreed that the winner at

Winged Foot would be under par. Dad took out his fat money clip and threw it on the big corner table. "I'm taking all bets," he shouted. "Nobody breaks par." When Hale Irwin won with a seven-over-par score, Dad collected more than two grand, a fact the board of directors found unsettling, to say the least.

Even though Craig, Dick, and I were out on our own, we knew things weren't the same as they had been before. Dad continued to serve the old members as he always had. But as for the new members, the Westchester blue bloods who went straight from Choate to Columbia to the first tee of the West Course, Dad didn't hold the door for many of those guys. When one of his old buddies suggested that he make an effort to meet some of the new members, Dad shrugged and went back to his office. He couldn't have cared less.

We weren't surprised when, in the early eighties, Dad's contracts with Winged Foot and Thunderbird were not renewed. What we didn't fully comprehend at the time was how Dad's departure from those jobs marked the end of an era. He was the last major champion who was also a club pro, closing the door on a part of the game that went back more than a hundred years. With his quiet dismissal, the days of the player–club pro came to a quiet and uneventful close.

Thankfully, Dad still had friends. His Majesty offered to move Dad to Morocco and take care of him for the rest of his life, an offer he repeated many times for the rest of Dad's life. Dad might have taken him up on it if a group of friends from Winged Foot and Texas hadn't gotten together and offered Dad a job as the teaching professional at Lochinvar, an exclusive private club in Houston that catered primarily to oilmen. Dad accepted and moved to Texas.

It was his second stint in the Lone Star State. When Jimmy Demaret was drafted into the navy during World War II, he phoned Dad and asked him to take his job as head professional at River Oaks, a club where my brother Dick would later serve as the head professional. Oddly enough, I would also spend many years in Houston, starting when I moved in with Dick and worked for Dave Marr, and going on to work at Lochinvar, both when Dad was there and afterward. This was ironic given how much I had hated Texas when I first moved to the University of Houston as a brash, hotheaded teenager. The second time I lived there, I loved it and continue to love it to this day. Dad had stayed in Texas only six months his first time around. His second stint lasted nine years.

Maybe it was the warm weather, the vastness of the state, or the can-do caring attitude of the Texans who stepped up when he needed them most, but Dad began pulling himself together. For the rest of his life he would thank his friends for helping him when he was down, just as I and my brothers have remembered the men and women in our lives to whom we owe an immeasurable debt of gratitude.

I tell my father's story to all my tour players to pound home the message that if you take care of the people around you, they will take care of you. So far, all of them have stepped up. The week after Tiger won his first U.S. Open at Pebble Beach, he traveled to Las Vegas to caddy for his good friend Jerry Chang in qualifying for the U.S. Public Links Championship. Tiger never forgot his friends, and he did everything he could for them, including sneaking across the fence on the second hole and taking Jerry's bag so as not to become a distraction during warm-ups.

After the round, I took Tiger, Jerry, and a few friends out to dinner at The Palm restaurant in Las Vegas, where the owners had set aside a private room for us in the back. After dinner as we were preparing to leave, Tiger let everyone else go out first in case he was mobbed for autographs. The patrons at The Palm didn't mob him; they did something else—they all stopped eating and applauded as Tiger walked out.

It was one of the nicest things I've ever seen a crowd of people do in a public place, and a sign of the respect everyone has for Tiger. I respected him as well that night, not for what he'd done at Pebble Beach but for humbling himself and caddying for a friend the day after that historic victory.

My brother Billy has a similar friendship with Jay Haas. Even though they have worked together in a player-caddy and player-coach capacity for many years, it is their friendship that both men value more than their professional successes. For example, one of Billy's sons is named Jay and one of Jay's is named Billy. That sort of bond extends far beyond the professional realm.

Because they are so close, they have had one of the longest-lasting player-coach-caddy relationships in the game, even when Billy was going through some of the more difficult times in his life battling addition, and when Jay was going through dry spells on tour. At the 1994 Masters, with eighteen to play, Jay was in the hunt with a chance to win his first major. At the par-five fifteenth, he hit a good tee shot and had 263 yards to the green. Throughout the week, Jay and Billy had decided that 259 yards was their cut-off point for going for the green. If they were inside 259, Jay would go for it; if they were outside that yardage, he would lay up. But Billy knew that he needed to go for it. This was the best chance he'd had in years to win a major, and those opportunities don't come along too often. A birdie gave them a chance. An eagle put them squarely in the hunt.

"What is it, Billy?" Jay asked.

At the moment of truth, Billy lied. "Two-fifty-eight," he said. "Hit it solid."

Jay hit a perfect three-wood right at the flag, and the first words out of Billy's mouth were, "Get up!"

Jay said, "Don't worry, I got all of it."

Billy said to himself, "Yeah, but I didn't *give* all of it."

The ball landed on the front of the green, and rolled just beyond the flag. Jay made birdie and finished fifth behind eventual winner José Maria Olazábal.

The next week, Billy's conscience got the best of him. As he and Jay were walking down the tenth fairway at Harbour Town Links on Hilton Head Island, Billy said, "Jay, I've got something to tell you."

Jay said, "You gonna confess to shorting that distance on fifteen?"

"You knew?"

"I knew exactly where the marker was," Jay said. "And I know why you did it. Thanks. Just don't do it again."

They have remained the best of friends for more than two decades because there is nothing that they wouldn't do for each other.

"Treat people like you would want to be treated if you were in their shoes, and word will spread that you're a good guy," Dad would say. "If you treat little people as if they're little, your reputation will be ruined inside a year."

If my students don't learn anything else from me, I hope they learn that one.

CLAUDE'S PEARLS

● Always be a giver no matter how much you have to give.

● If you take care of everyone you meet, you never have to worry about whom you might have slighted along the way.

● Friendship is precious, and too often rare. Work to keep your friends close.

● It doesn't cost a dime to be nice. You don't have to be rich, or smart, or funny. If you're nice, people will remember you. And if you're not nice, they will also remember you.

"Stop Worrying About the Socks"

At the 1983 Masters, Billy walked onto the lawn of the clubhouse and onto the driving range where he saw Dad chatting with a few of his old buddies. Like all retired past champions, Dad wore his Augusta National green jacket whenever he was on club grounds. As Billy walked by, he noticed that the club logo on Dad's green jacket was frayed, almost hanging off.

"Dad, look at your jacket," Billy said. "Can't you get that fixed? You're a past champion. Look at that. You should take care of that a little better."

Dad smiled and tugged on Billy's white jumpsuit, the one worn by all Augusta National caddies. He said, "You take care of that white tuxedo, son. I'll take care of the green jacket."

Billy recounts that story anytime someone starts nitpicking the small stuff. "You take care of that white tuxedo" was Dad's way of telling Billy, and us, to focus on the important things in life and stop sweating the nonessential details.

Dad wanted us all to know that family and friends were all that mattered, not the professional accomplishments or the trophies at home. All he wanted out of life was the knowledge that he had been good to his friends and that his children had been raised the right way.

As Dad got older and his arthritis worsened, doctors began to notice that his heart was enlarged. That led to more serious problems, problems that the doctors weren't sure they could ever cure. The news had the typical effect: Dad suffered from bouts of depression. Sometimes he would have to be hospitalized for arrhythmia, but also for the blues that accompanied his ailments. Dad's life well lived had caught up with him in the end, and his health failed rapidly throughout the late eighties.

During one particularly bad time in early 1989, one of the members at Lochinvar picked up the phone and called Mr. Hogan at his office in Fort Worth. When his secretary heard that it was about Claude Harmon's health, she put the call through. The member told Mr. Hogan that Dad had grown depressed and had given up. Some speculated that he might not live another week.

Mr. Hogan had a business to run, one of the most successful golf club companies in the world at that time; he had meetings to attend and calls to return; he had to go to Shady Oaks, his golf club in Fort Worth, for lunch, as he did every day; and he had to be home by nightfall or Valerie, who became extremely protective of him in the later years, would worry. None of that mattered. Mr. Hogan dropped everything, hopped into his Cadillac, and drove from Fort Worth to Houston (a monumental event in and of itself, since Mr. Hogan drove very little after his accident). Once there, he marched past the nurses' station and went straight to my father's bedside.

"Get up, Claude," Mr. Hogan said without preamble. "I've driven all the way down here to see you. You're not going to lay in that bed, are you?"

Dad crept out of the bed, and inched his way into a nearby chair.

"I hear you've given up," Mr. Hogan said. "I hear you don't want to live anymore. When I heard that I said, 'That can't be. Claude Harmon's never given up on anything.' So, I came down here to see for myself. What's it going to be, Claude? Have you given up? If so, just go ahead and die right here with me watching. If not, you need to get up and get going."

Dad got up, and lived another six months.

During those final six months of his life, with his heart growing larger and weaker by the day, he made a point of giving each of us a final lesson—one memory that would stick. Mine came only a couple of days before Dad passed away. In the last stages of his sickness, Dad had five tubes in his diaphragm and weighed less than at any time in his adult life. We took turns sitting up with him in the hospital, and after dinner one night, when it was only the two of us in the room, he turned his head on the pillow and looked at me.

The eyes weren't as sharp as they had been, and his expressions had long ago eased in intensity. "I've got something to talk to you about," he said.

My first thought was, "What have I done now? On his deathbed and he's going to give me one last lecture."

"You know, I was a lot more like you than you'll ever know," he said. "I skipped school every time I could get away with it, and did just enough to get by. And I was just as pigheaded as you.

Once I made my mind up about something, nobody was going to change it, even if I was wrong."

I slumped back in my chair with my jaw hanging down. These words couldn't have been coming from my father. This was the man who, as far as I could tell, had been born a responsible adult. To hear him admit to making many of my own mistakes seemed surreal.

He took a couple of deep breaths before continuing. Then he looked at me again and said, "I didn't always show it, but I always respected the fact that you never wavered once you'd made your mind up about something. Now, you were wrong a lot of the time, but I still respected your passion. You remind me a lot of me, good and bad. I'm proud of that, and I'm proud of you, son, and I love you very much."

One final lesson from the man who taught me everything.

For Billy, the final lesson came in the form of a watch. Like me, my father always owned fine watches—Rolexes, mostly. This had started when he worked for the King of Morocco. His Majesty and Dad had birthdays a week apart, so Dad would make a special trip to Rabat every July for a giant birthday bash. The king was very generous. Our homes were always furnished with fine Moroccan antiques and rugs, and Dad always had a new gold Rolex on his arm—birthday gifts from the King that he cherished.

During one of his rebellious rants with Dad, Billy had tried to throw out the most hurtful line he could. "You know, you don't care about anything or anybody," he said. "To you, life is nothing but a new gold Rolex watch." Billy regretted those words for twenty years.

Then, as Dad lay dying in the hospital, he called Billy into his room and said, "Son, I've got a few things I want to talk to you about."

"Okay, Dad," Billy said, not knowing what to expect.

Dad motioned toward the door where Billy's wife had just left to go to the commissary for a bite to eat. "You've got a great girl out there," he said. "Don't screw it up."

But he didn't say "screw." It was the first time Billy had ever heard my father drop the F-bomb. It was not something he did often, and never in front of us, even when we were adults. "You're right, Dad," Billy said. "She is something special. And I plan to do whatever it takes to keep her."

Dad nodded and said, "You know, son, as I lay here, I don't think about any of the golf tournaments I won, or the course records I set, or the great jobs I had. All that matters when you're right here is the people you love and the friends you've made. As you go through life, remember that. Don't let the things you won't care about when you're right here . . ." he slapped the sheets of his hospital bed, "get between you and the people you love."

Billy had trouble speaking at that point, but he nodded while biting his lip and lowering his eyes to regain his composure.

"And one more thing . . ." he said.

"Yes, Dad."

"I lived a pretty full life, and the family lived full lives, so unfortunately I didn't leave a lot behind for you kids. But I do have something special that I want to give you."

He reached into the nightstand, brought out a small box, opened it, and laughed as he gave Billy a new Rolex. "I've waited twenty years for this," he said. "I knew I'd have to wait until I was on my deathbed to get you back for that one. But I know you don't like gold, so I got you a platinum Rolex."

Billy had one more great moment with Dad, but only because he was in the hospital room answering the phone one night in Dad's final week. When one caller asked to speak with Claude Harmon, Billy said, "Who's calling?"

"Ben Hogan."

At first Billy thought it was a crank call. He started to say, "Yeah, right, and I'm Jack Nicklaus," but something about the voice made him hand the phone to Dad.

It was indeed Mr. Hogan. Dad took the phone, said hello, and immediately sat a little straighter. A smile broke across his frail face, and his voice picked up a notch. He and Mr. Hogan talked for almost an hour, mostly about golf, but also about family and life. The week before, Keith Clearwater had shot a pair of sixty-fours on the weekend at Colonial to win the golf tournament. Mr. Hogan held the record for most tournament wins at Colonial, a club where he had practiced and played for many years, so he, better than anyone, knew how impressive 128 was on that course. Dad said, "The game is a lot different now than it was when you and I were playing."

Mr. Hogan said, "It should be, Claude. If the players today weren't better than we were, then we wouldn't have done our jobs. I think we've left it in pretty good shape."

"I think you're right, Ben," Dad said. "I guess guys like you and me are gray men, black-and-white photos hanging on clubhouse walls."

"Well, I don't know about that," Mr. Hogan said. "My favorite color's red."

Dad laughed and looked more alive than he had in weeks.

Then after a long pause, Mr. Hogan said, "Claude, I just want you to know you're one of the best friends I ever had."

Dad chuckled again, and said, "Well, hell, Ben, it's a short list."

A few minutes later, they said goodbye and Dad hung up the phone. It was the last time he would speak to his good friend.

I spoke to Mr. Hogan a week later. On Monday, August 21, 1989, my father passed away in his hospital bed in Houston, with his family by his side. After contacting our extended relatives, one of the first calls I made was to Mr. Hogan's office.

"Butch, how are you?" he said. "How's your father?"

"Mr. Hogan, that's the reason I've called. I just wanted you to know before you heard it from someone else that Dad passed away today."

For several seconds the only sound was Mr. Hogan's sniffles. Then he said, "I'm so sorry to hear that. You know, your father meant a lot to me. If there's anything I can do for you or your family, please let me know."

There was one final lesson, though, one we would all remember. It was my father's last message to my brother Dick. After retiring from Lochinvar and moving into a condo near Dick's home, Dad visited Dick often, coming out to River Oaks for lunch several times a week and hanging out in the locker room where he would entertain the members with his stories. The members loved him, and they were thrilled whenever he made an appearance. Dick wasn't quite as enthusiastic.

Dick stocked cashmere socks—expensive things—for his affluent members, and Dad helped himself every time he passed through. Whenever Billy was in Houston, Dad would make a point of taking him out to River Oaks to see Dick. Dad would hook his arm through Billy's as they walked through the golf shop. Then he would say, "Watch what Dick does when I take these socks. It tears him up."

Sure enough, Dick would fume and fuss, and say to me, "Can you believe he just takes those socks?"

"Have you said anything to him about it?" I asked.

"Of course not. You know what he would say."

"Yeah, he'd tell you to get over yourself."

"But he just helps himself. Those are expensive socks. How many pair does the man need?"

When Dad passed away, Dick went to his condo to pick out a suit for the funeral. As he rummaged through his closet, overwhelmed with emotion, he ran across several boxes. When Dick opened the boxes, he fell against the closet wall and broke down. They were full of unopened, unwrapped, and unworn cashmere socks.

"He never even opened them," Dick choked out to me later that day. "He never wore them. He took them, and put them up."

"He didn't want them," I told him. "He only took them because he knew it bugged you. It was his way of telling you not to sweat the small stuff. That's your final lesson from Dad: stop worrying about the socks."

That afternoon I realized something, and it brought a smile to my tight, worn face: Dad never stopped teaching, even after he was gone.

CLAUDE'S PEARLS

- If you're going to criticize others, make sure you've taken a long look in the mirror ahead of time.

- Don't worry about the things that won't matter to you on your deathbed.

- Get over yourself. Your pet peeves are just that: yours. Nobody else cares.

- And don't let anything get in between you and the people you love. Because in the end, they're all that matters.

Epilogue

MOVING FORWARD

On the back of the driving range at the TPC at Sawgrass during the Tuesday practice session before the Players Championship, Lee Janzen asked me to work with him. I had a pretty full stable at the time and hadn't planned on taking on any additional players, but I liked Lee, knew his game, and thought I could help him. So I spent a couple of hours with him working on getting his hands in a good position at the top, which allowed him to square the clubface more consistently. About an hour into the session, he reverted to his old swing and hit a weak push-cut. Trying to find some positive, he said, "Well, that's not great, but I could play it."

I laughed and said, "That wasn't worth crap. Maybe some other guy will blow smoke up your butt and tell you that you can play with that, but not me. I don't want to see you hit that shot again."

It was not what he expected, but he appreciated my brutal honesty, as do all of my players. That's the one trait of my father's I'm glad I inherited. If you don't want to hear it straight, go somewhere else. Because the Harmons tell it like it is without any window dressing. We are all pathological truth-tellers—just like our father.

My life is as fulfilled now as it has ever been. Reaching this stage in my profession after tumbling as far as I had reminds me of another of Dad's sayings: "Make sure that what you do reflects who you are. If you do that, success will take care of itself." My brothers and I have achieved great success in our profession. But we've also discovered great success in life. Christy and I have a wonderful life together in Las Vegas where I have my golf schools. My son Claude III has become a prominent teacher in Austin, Texas. My daughter, Michaele, and I are as close as we've ever been, and my eleven-year-old son Cole keeps me young and energetic. My list of students is strong. My golf schools are full. And I get together with my brothers two or three times a year, when we share family stories and good times.

Craig is one of the greatest club professionals in the nation, the recipient of many PGA of America awards and someone whom the members at Oak Hill continue to admire and appreciate. When he retires, they will have to hire three pros to replace him. He still teaches a number of outstanding players, and he hosts PGA teaching seminars across the country, where he will invariably get into at least one disagreement with his brothers.

Before his untimely passing, Dick lived in Houston, where he opened the Dick Harmon Golf Schools, a successful teaching facility that attracts some of the top players in the world. In addition to coaching players like Craig Stadler, Dick was known for his ability to communicate with talented junior golfers. He was the best in the business when it came to spotting young talent.

But of the entire Harmon family, the greatest success story has to be my brother Billy. Without a doubt, Billy was the most talented junior golfer in our family, but as I've said, he also became an alcoholic and drug addict, and came close to losing everything. As he tells it, "I was getting loaded every day, which is a pretty good indication that you have a problem. But there was always a time when I was going to quit. I was going to quit when I got this or that job, or I was going to quit when I got married, or when Dad died. When we had a child I was going to stop, but I never did. I was a functioning addict, the pro at Newport Country Club and the teaching professional at The Vintage, two of the best jobs in the country, but in my eyes I could not have been more worthless."

Billy had a lovely home in Newport, Rhode Island, but in his study, which had a beautiful bay window overlooking the ocean, he had turned the television and chair away from the window to shut out the world. Beside him sat a TV tray that was always stocked with ice, glasses, and plenty of booze.

"Everybody has a different bottom," he says. "Mine came when my son was two months old. He woke up crying, needing to be fed, and my wife got up and fed him, as she'd done every night since he had been born. I remember lying in bed being angry that he had woken me up—because I was loaded, as always. That's when it hit me. I said to myself, 'You know, if she weren't here, you couldn't take care of your own son because you're a drunk. Getting drunk and using is more important to you than your own child.' At that moment, if I'd had a gun I would have shot myself. That was bottom."

Within a month, friends and family put together an intervention, and Billy got the help he needed. He hasn't had a drink since. As he says, "I have realized that my son might never see me drunk, and that is the greatest feeling I've ever had."

I know that the day Billy asked for help and went to his first meeting, Mom and Dad were somewhere shedding tears of joy and pride, just as they had done when he won his first big golf tournament, and just as we all were when he decided to put his life back together.

My family means more to me than anything else, and the respect and love of my brothers is what I long for these days. I guess the lessons Claude Harmon, Sr., taught us all those years about what is truly important in life have finally taken root.

I think about Dad at special times—like when I get phone messages from Ben Crane, who called me shedding tears of joy after he won his first tour event in Atlanta—and at simple times like a Vegas sunset when my son and I are on the range together. I think about him when I look at the wall in my office and see the photo of him holding me in his arms, moments after he and Pete Cooper won the Miami Fourball, or when I see the framed cover of *Sports Illustrated* from April 27, 1964, with a picture of Dad beneath the headline "Let Me Help Your Game: A New Instructional Series by Famed Instructor Claude Harmon." I think about him whenever I'm doing a shoot or an article for *Golf Digest*. In fact, in November 1997 I did a cover shot for that magazine: I was hitting a sand shot with one hand, under the headline "Get Out of the Sand with One Hand, by Butch Harmon." I have it framed on the wall next to another issue of *Golf Digest*, this one from September 1972, with my father on the cover shown hitting a sand shot with one hand beneath the same headline. There is nothing in this game that I didn't learn from him, and nothing in life that I don't owe exclusively to his wisdom.

Perhaps the fondest memory I have of my time with Tiger came at Pebble Beach in 2000, when he won the U.S. Open in record fashion. As he was walking up the eighteenth fairway on

Sunday, my brother Dick called my brother Billy and asked the question we were all thinking and the one that brought out the emotion in each of us. "I was just wondering, Billy," Dick said. "What do you think Dad would say to Butch today?"

Billy never got to answer. He was too overwhelmed. And when I saw him afterward, I was too emotional to say much, either.

October 2005 was a great month for the Harmon family. The third week of that month, my student José Maria Olazábal won the Mallorca Classic, his first European Tour title of the year and one of the most special for him, since it came in his home country of Spain. That same week, Jay Haas, who continues to call Billy his teacher and friend, won the SBC Championship, one of the biggest events of the year on the Champions Tour; and Lucas Glover, a great kid from Greenville, South Carolina, who is coached by Dick Harmon, sank a shot from the bunker on the final hole to win his first tour event at Walt Disney World and earn a spot in the season-ending Tour Championship. We razzed Craig for the next month, telling everyone that the same week three of the Harmon brothers had players win on tours around the world, Craig's star pupil, a Mrs. O'Shannahan, broke a hundred for the first time.

But what happened two weeks later made our three players winning in the same week seem almost insignificant. I got the news on a Tuesday afternoon while I was standing on the driving range at East Lake Golf Club in Atlanta, the classic old Donald Ross course where Bobby Jones played his first and last rounds of golf. The place oozes history. Bobby Jones's old locker still sits in the clubhouse, which, itself, looks as it did in 1930. Players love the place, not just because of the history and the classic feel of the golf course but also because since 2001 East Lake has been the permanent home of the Tour Championship, the season-ending event on the PGA Tour for the top-thirty money winners. To get there, you had to have had a pretty good year.

I stood on the range, arms folded across my chest, watching as Adam Scott hit one pitching-wedge shot after another to a target on the left side of the range. We were working on moving the club down the target line prior to impact rather than having it come from an inside plane. After impact, we wanted his arms to move left around his body instead of separating from his torso and extending down the target line. A lot of people work on the opposite, trying to deliver the club from an inside plane and then extend the arms toward the target. Unfortunately, the ball's gone after impact, so any extension down the line in the followthrough does not affect ball flight, and delivering the club from an inside path requires you to clear your hips through impact, a motion not conducive to hitting precise wedge shots. For a player who generates a lot of clubhead speed, as Adam does, delivering the club down the target line allows you to control distance and trajectory, especially with wedge shots where distance, trajectory, and spin are vital to hitting the ball close to the hole.

To my right, Davis Love III was working on a similar motion with a five-iron. Jack Lumpkin, one of Dad's former assistants who now teaches Davis and many other great players, held a club chest high over the ball with the shaft pointing well left of the target. This gave Davis a visual cue to move his arms left after impact. I couldn't help smiling. We were both teaching a technique my father had taught to us—one that produced maximum distance and control in 1945 and in 2005.

A moment after Adam hit a perfect, low-spin wedge shot that hit just short of his target and hopped forward to within a couple of inches of the hole, my cell phone vibrated in my pocket. Carrying phones on the course during tournament play is strictly forbidden, but on Tuesdays and Wednesdays I take and receive no fewer than thirty calls on the course and range as I work with different players. This particular Tuesday I had already taken calls from Fred Couples, Natalie Gulbis, my wife, my secretary, and Bob Chiles, the man who makes my belts. So I didn't hesitate to answer when I saw my brother Craig's number on the display screen.

"I've got some great news," Craig said.

"You had another student break a hundred," I said.

"No, even better: Dad just got elected into the Teachers Hall of Fame."

"Well, it's about damn time!"

That outburst caught everybody's attention. Adam and Davis stopping hitting balls and turned around, and Jack dropped the club he was holding and gave me a "What's that all about?" look.

I hung up with Craig and said, "Dad just made it into the Teachers Hall of Fame."

They all nodded. Then Jack said, "He's been on my ballot every year for the last twenty years. I guess enough of us finally wrote him in that they couldn't ignore us."

"It's a shame it took so long," I said. Dad had been dead sixteen years.

"That's right," Jack said. "I don't think he was any better a teacher this year than he was last."

We both laughed. Then Davis, whose father is also in the Hall, said, "Congratulations. It's well deserved."

That it was. And I know that somewhere my dad appreciated the compliment as much as I did.

* * *

Whenever I'm sitting in my office reflecting on all that my father did for my brothers and me, I open my desk drawer and pull out an old copy of a poem that Winged Foot member Bill DiGiacomo wrote about Dad just before he moved to Texas. It goes:

Proey at Winged Foot
And there's almost an Open
East and West sixty-ones
Yet to be broken

A sixty at Seminole
An Augustan Green Coat
Golf Knight of Morocco
A tempo without choke

A pro for all seasons
In winter, Palm Springs
Many yarns at the bar
The good and bad swings

The Master of sand
In no rough he enters
Left hip that slides
To trounce the weekenders

A professor of swings
To pros and the duffer
A pro who makes pros
To Hogan, "Jolly Golfer."

He meant a lot to a lot of people. And he meant the world to all of his sons.

My brothers and I visited Winged Foot together not long ago. We are still members there, and we try to get to the club anytime we are all in New York. During this visit, as we were sitting at Dad's old table in the grillroom, a friend of the family came up and reminisced for a few minutes. Then the man said, "You know, I loved your dad, but I always thought he was awfully hard on you boys."

I thought about that for a second. Then I said, "He was. He was very hard on us. And look how we all turned out. I guess he knew what he was doing after all."

I can only hope to be half the teacher, half the father, and half the man I found in The Pro, the man whose name I share.

Appendix

TIGER: THEN AND NOW

I've already talked extensively about the changes made to Tiger Woods's swing after his 1997 Masters victory. What I haven't discussed, until now, are the changes I see in Tiger's swing since he and I stopped working together.

The first thing you should know about Tiger Woods is that I believe he can win swinging the club a lot of different ways. I think if you told him that he had to swing with a couple of loops in his backswing, Tiger would figure out a way to get it done and win. His talent is such that he can win when he is swinging good, when he's swinging not so good, and when his swing is in transition. He is the most coordinated and naturally gifted athlete in our sport. He is also very much like Jack Nicklaus, in that he figures out a way to win even when his game isn't hitting on all cylinders. If he's spraying his tee shots, he figures out a way to recover from the rough and make enough birdies to win. If he's missing greens, he figures out how to hole it from the fringe or the bunkers. If he's not putting well, he just hits it closer. Whatever it takes to shoot the lowest number, Tiger figures it out. He's the best since Nicklaus at keeping himself in the game even when he doesn't have his best stuff.

One of the reasons I believe Tiger felt he needed to change his swing was longer driving distance. When he first turned pro, Tiger drove it past everybody by a healthy margin. Davis Love and John Daly were close, but no one consistently hit it as far and in as many fairways as did Tiger. When he needed to blast it past an opponent, he had that ability. Then, starting about 2001, players started catching up with him. Ernie Els, Phil Mickelson, and Vijay Singh all started hitting the ball close to, if not as long as, Tiger, and occasionally those players and others hit it by him. He never admitted it, but I believe that bothered him. He knew he generated more clubhead speed than anyone else out there—he had gotten even faster since he'd started working out in his mid-twenties—so being challenged off the tee was not something that was supposed to happen. When it did, I think he decided he needed to make some changes.

I believe that Tiger's perceived loss of distance (or the fact that the rest of the tour started catching up to him in the distance category) had more to do with his equipment than his golf swing. He insisted on staying with a 43¾-inch steel-shafted driver with a smaller head while his fellow competitors were playing 45-inch graphite shafts and jumbo titanium heads. It's hard to question Tiger's reluctance to make a dramatic equipment change. He was the best player in the world. Tossing your driver when you're playing great is a tough thing to do. There were plenty of graphite shafts Tiger could have hit, but he took a cautious approach to change. No one can fault him for that decision. But I think overhauling his golf swing was a mistake when putting a new driver in the bag would have done the trick.

A novice can look at Tiger's swing today compared to his incredible run in 2000 and tell that there is a difference. He doesn't swing the same way now as he did then. What most amateurs can't recognize is exactly where the swings differ and why. The main difference between Tiger's old swing and his new one is the plane on which the club travels.

(As an aside for those who don't understand what "swing plane" means, the plane of the swing is simply the geometric plane that would form if you marked dots in space at every point the club traveled during the swing and connected those dots into a solid "plane," like an imaginary wall or pane of glass. If you've watched any televised golf in the last couple of years, you've seen various swing planes through stop-action and computer-animated coloring.)

In Tiger's case, swing plane is critical because his swing speed is at least 50 percent greater than that of the average amateur. A tenth of a degree variance in the position of his clubface or the path of the swing at impact can mean the difference between finding the fairway and having to yell "Fore right!" When we worked together, I believed that the best way for Tiger to control his distance and direction was for him to keep the club moving square to the target line for as long as possible. This required a more vertical swing plane, where the club stayed in front of his chest and his right elbow never got behind his body, and a backswing where the club rarely reached parallel.

Today, Tiger's swing plane is about twenty degrees more horizontal than it was when we were working together. By putting the club on this slightly flatter plane and making his swing longer than it was in 2000 and 2001, Tiger hits the ball farther now than at any other time in his life. He can also spray the driver much farther off line than he ever did during his record-setting run. If you look closely at Tiger's swing then and now, you can see that there is more power in today's motion, but the opportunity for error is also greater.

By getting the club on the slightly rounder plane, Tiger has, on occasion, worked the club down toward the ball rather than out toward the target. When this happens, his head dips; the club-face never squares up; and the ball goes a zillion miles right of target. You don't have to hit more than one or two of those wide, right foul balls before you start overcompensating to correct, and you pull a couple of shots. Now, as Tiger gets more comfortable, those errors happen less often and he wins the way he won in 1997, 1999, and 2000—by overpowering the field. When you hit a nine-iron or wedge into every par four and hit every par five in two, the game is a lot easier than if you're trying to work three-, four-, or five-irons close to the pins. Tiger's new swing affords him the luxury of missing a few fairways because he's so long; he often hits it past bunkers or beyond the hazards that ensnarl humans of normal ability. He hits it so long and makes so many birdies that it's easy for him to say, "So what if I hit one fifty yards off line."

I disagree with that philosophy—I think it's better to be a little shorter and in the middle of the fairway than long and in the rough—but that's not news to Tiger. Ben Hogan taught that lesson to my father, and my father taught it to me: you can control your approach from the fairway, even if you're a little farther away from the hole. Tiger and I had this discussion many times, and we have chosen to disagree. I'm not the one hitting the shots, so his opinion is the only one that counts. And he continues to hit some awfully good golf shots.

So is Tiger's old swing better than his new one? Was I right?

Or has his current success proved that he was right and I was wrong? I think the answers are: no, no, and no. The new swing is no better or worse than the old one; it's simply different. Tiger played great with the swing we built, and he's playing great with the one he's built in the last few years. That's the way golf works. Neither of us was right or wrong; we simply approached the same objective from different angles.

In the end, all the matters are the numbers on the scoreboard. And as long as Tiger Woods continues to post lower numbers than the other players in the game, he will continue to be the number-one golfer in the world and an athlete for the ages.

In Memoriam: Dick Harmon

The first week of February 2006, my brother Dick was in Palm Springs visiting with my brother Billy and his family. Two weeks before, all four Harmon brothers had been together at Tuscana Golf Club in Indian Wells, California, the first time any of us had done a golf school together. The next day, I chartered a plane to Orlando, where we attended Dad's induction into the Teacher's Hall of Fame. The day after the ceremony, Dick, Billy, and I flew to Orlando for the PGA Merchandise show where we had dinner and drinks and shared a lot of laughs. It's always great to be with my brothers, but this was a particularly special time. Not only were we celebrating Dad's induction, all of us were excited about the impending publication of the book you now hold. Billy, Dick, and Craig spent a lot of hours helping me pull together the memories in these pages, and talking about those memories brought us closer together than ever before. After the Orlando show, I went home to Las Vegas, and Dick when to California.

On the second Friday of February, Dick decided to go to the Eisenhower Medical Center, not far from Billy's house, for a nagging cough and shortness of breath brought on by walking pneumonia that had been bothering him for several days. Billy went with him. Any trip to the hospital is cause for concern, but nobody was expecting terrible news. Unfortunately, while in the hospital, Dick suffered a massive cardiac arrest. He died suddenly and unexpectedly that morning with Billy nearby.

The shock of Dick's death is hard to describe. When I got the call, I couldn't believe that my little brother, my best friend in life, my teacher, and the man who had been there for me when I had nowhere else to turn, was gone. Later, after the numbness of shock gave way to the warm sorrow of grief, I realized that the people who would miss my brother the most might well have been golfers, but the reasons that Dick would be missed had nothing to do with golf. Dick Harmon was, above all else, a giver. He didn't just listen to Dad's edict about always being a giver and not a taker; he lived that lesson every day of his life. He was a teacher of the young, and a sage for the old; a friend to many, and an enemy of none.

At Dick's memorial service we were all understandably emotional. As the eldest, I always assumed my younger siblings would outlive me, and I certainly wasn't prepared for Dick to pass away. I told Billy, "You know, you and I have screwed up enough and ticked off enough people in our lives that we deserve to have enemies. But I don't know a soul who knew Dick who didn't think the world of him. If you didn't like Dick Harmon, something was wrong with you."

This book was meant to be a story of a Pro, a man who left an indelible imprint on golf, but whose legacy affected things far more important than a game. In that effort I hope I have succeeded, not just in showing the grace and character of Claude Harmon, but of his son Dick as well.

Dick Harmon joined our parents on February 10, 2006. He left behind a wife, Nancy, four children, two sisters, and three brothers who will miss him more than he will ever know.

We love you, Dickie. Keep Dad in line till we get there.

Acknowledgments

I can only imagine what my dad would say if he were around today to see the book you're holding. He would probably point his finger at me and say, "You wrote this?" to which I would say, "Yes." Then he'd no doubt grunt, and say, "Well, that answers one question: I wasn't sure you'd ever read a book, but I guess you had to read this one if you wrote it."

That's when I would have to admit to Dad that I had plenty of help in putting this book together. Even though golf is a solitary sport, few have ever advanced very far in the game without help from others. The same is true of writing. This work was a group effort that wouldn't have been possible without the herculean efforts of some great people. First, I want to thank my brothers, Craig, Dick, and Billy, for all the time they devoted to this book. If I didn't know it before, I know now that their memories are better than mine. Also, I owe a great debt of gratitude to the members and friends of Winged Foot Golf Club who kindly opened their archives and helped in more ways than I can mention. In particular, I want to thank my good friends Jack L. Copeland, Douglas Larue Smith, and Tom Leslie, who went above and beyond the call to make sure the club did everything in its power to make this book a success. Thanks also to my good friends at *Golf Digest*.

Then there were the mechanical engineers who walked me through the writing and publishing process: my agents, Rocky Hambric and Mark Reiter; my collaborator, Steve Eubanks; my editor, Luke Dempsey; and our publisher, Steve Ross. Thanks to all. Also a special thanks to Jackie Burke, Jack Lumpkin, Fred Couples, Jay Haas, and everyone else who knew my father and encouraged me to tell his story.

Finally, I have to thank my wife, Christy, for her encouragement, her devotion, and most of all her love.

Index

NOTE: CH refers to Claude Harmon; BH refers to Butch Harmon.